THE DRIVERS OF NASCAR

 **2006 EDITION**

BEN WHITE and **NIGEL KINRADE**

CRESTLINE

First published in 2006 by Crestline, an imprint of MBI Publishing Company, Galtier Plaza, Suite 200, 380 Jackson Street, St. Paul, MN 55101-3885 USA

This publication has been prepared solely by MBI Publishing Company. NASCAR and NASCAR Library Collection are registered trademarks of the National Association for Stock Car Auto Racing, Inc. We recognize that some words, model names, and designations mentioned herein are the property of the trademark holder. We use them for identification purposes only.

Crestline titles are also available at discounts in bulk quantity for industrial or sales-promotional use. For details, please contact: Special Sales Manager at MBI Publishing Company, Galtier Plaza, Suite 200, 380 Jackson Street, St. Paul, MN 55101-3885 USA.

For a free catalog, call 1-800-826-6600, or visit our website at www.motorbooks.com.

ISBN-13: 978-0-681-45450-7
ISBN-10: 0-681-45450-4

Printed in China

NASCAR® and NASCAR® Library Collection are registered trademarks of the National Association for Stock Car Auto Racing, Inc.

On the front cover: Tony Stewart, Matt Kenseth, Jeff Gordon, Jimmie Johnson.

On the back cover, top: Jeremy Mayfield. **Bottom:** Kasey Khane, Dale Earnhardt Jr.

Editors: Heather Oakley and Nicole Edman
Designer: Brenda C. Canales

CONTENTS

ACKNOWLEDGMENTS

First and foremost, I would like to thank the NASCAR NEXTEL Cup drivers and teams featured in this book for the time they extended to me for this project, as well as others projects I've written involving them over 23 years of motorsports journalism. Your continued friendships are most appreciated.

A tremendous thanks to Mike Mooney, John Dunlap, Crystal Carraway, Becky Cox, and the entire staff of NEXTEL for helping to provide information about each driver featured here.

Special thanks to Nigel Kinrade for his fantastic photographs, all of which are so important to this book. Nicole Edman of MBI Publishing Company offered tremendous contributions toward making this book a success.

As always, I'd like to thank Mark Ashenfelter, Kenny Bruce, Jon Gunn, Mike Hembree, Jeff Owens, Bob Pockrass, Adam Richardson, Ray Shaw, Whitney Shaw, Kirk Shaw, Steve Waid, Art Weinstein, and Rea White of *NASCAR Illustrated* and *NASCAR Scene* for their continued friendship and advice.

Kevin Harvick, driver of the RCR Enterprises Chevrolet, takes the checkered flag at Bristol Motor Speedway on April 3, 2005. It was his only NASCAR NEXTEL Cup win of the season.

Finally, I dedicate this book to my son, Aaron. You truly are my hero. Thanks for helping to make NASCAR NEXTEL Cup racing so enjoyable for me.

The cars driven by Kevin Harvick (29), Jamie McMurray (42), and David Stremme (14) make one of many crucial pit stops for tires and fuel.

Rusty Wallace, driver of the Penske Racing South Dodge, gets service from his crew during an event at Dover International Speedway in Dover, Delaware. In the two Dover events in 2005, Wallace finished fifth and third.

INTRODUCTION

Few of us get to experience the heart-pounding thrill of pushing a top-of-the-line stock car to its limits around a racetrack. Fewer still possess the elusive combination of skill, courage, and luck that it takes to be a NASCAR winner. As a result, millions of fans around the world look to these favored few as true heroes. So if fate hasn't seen fit to make us NASCAR NEXTEL Cup champions, then we should at least be able to sit down and chew the fat with our idols of the ovals.

Here we offer an up-close-and-personal look at the leading stock car drivers of our time. Some have faced both glory in the winner's circle and near-death encounters on the oval over lengthy, perhaps legendary, careers. Others are so young they barely look old enough to drive. Some come to the sport from veritable racing dynasties with winning pedigrees; others emerged from obscure beginnings and fought mightily just for the chance to prove themselves on the track. The highest of triumphs and lowest of disappointments can be seen in the eyes of these men and women, and their actions can be captured by the photographs on these pages.

Wherever they came from and whatever their background, all the men and women who slide through the window into the driver's seat of a NASCAR NEXTEL Cup car are motivated by the same force: the unrelenting desire to best a rival in a turn or down a straightaway and reach the finish line in front of the rest.

Tony Stewart (20) leads Bobby Labonte (18) and Brian Vickers (25) to the green flag at New Hampshire International Raceway. Stewart went on win the race.

MBV Motorsports teammates Scott Riggs (left), Boris Said (center), and Joe Nemchek (right) stop to pose for the cameras during a break in the action.

GREG BIFFLE

16

When talking about the NASCAR NEXTEL Cup drivers who are flashy and outspoken, Greg Biffle isn't one to be considered the life of the party. His manner is rather quiet, as he'd rather let his talents on the racetrack to do the talking.

Biffle, driver of the Roush Racing Ford, certainly did his fair share of communicating on the racetrack in 2005. He managed to collect wins at California in February, Darlington in May, and Dover and Michigan in June. Under the direction of championship-winning crew chief Doug Richert, the team showed a fair amount of strength.

On just as many occasions, they found themselves on the other end of the spectrum, with a 25th-place finish at Daytona, a 29th at Martinsville, a 41st at Phoenix, and a 38th at Watkins Glen.

Years of racing have taught Biffle that seasons can include both feast and famine when it comes to performance.

While progressing through the various levels of NASCAR racing before making his NASCAR NEXTEL Series Cup debut in 2002, his name continued to surface as a contender. But before that huge jump, Biffle logged championships in both the NASCAR Craftsman Truck Series in 2000 and the NASCAR Busch Series in 2002, as well as being Rookie of the Year in both divisions. He also ran seven 2002 NASCAR NEXTEL Cup events for team owners Andy Petree, Jack Roush, and Kyle Petty, gaining

Biffle takes his patriotic No. 16 National Guard Ford through its paces.

experience before his 2003 baptism into the most competitive form of auto racing in the world.

Biffle joined NASCAR's elite circuit in 2003 and, by July, scored a victory in the Pepsi 400 at Daytona International Speedway. That win served as a glimpse of good things to come, since a win in one's rookie season reveals a special talent just waiting to be unleashed. In August 2004, he scored a dominant victory at Michigan.

In 2005, Biffle easily secured a place in the Chase for the NASCAR NEXTEL Cup. Problems did prevail at times, mostly not of Biffle's doing.

"I don't know if we've had a lull or not, but this race team has a never-give-up attitude," Biffle says. "I'm real excited to get the National Guard car in victory lane. I know all of the soldiers over in Iraq watch the races. They can't wait to see NASCAR NEXTEL Series Cup racing on TV. It's really exciting to get them in victory lane."

Born:	December 23, 1969, Vancouver, Washington
Height:	5-9
Weight:	170 lbs

Sponsor	National Guard
Make	Ford
Crew Chief	Doug Richert
Team	Roush Racing

Greg Biffle raises his arms in celebration after winning a NASCAR NEXTEL Cup event at California in March 2005.

Biffle slides to a stop as his crew works at a fever pitch to change tires and add fuel to his No. 16 Roush Racing Ford.

NASCAR NEXTEL Cup Series Career Statistics

YEAR	RACES	WINS	TOP 5S	TOP 10S	POLES	TOTAL POINTS	FINAL STANDING	WINNINGS
2003	35	1	3	6	0	3,696	20th	$2,410,053
2004	36	2	4	8	1	3,902	17th	$4,092,877
2005	36	6	15	21	0	6498	2nd	$5,729,928
TOTALS	107	9	22	35	1	14,096		$12,232,858

MIKE BLISS

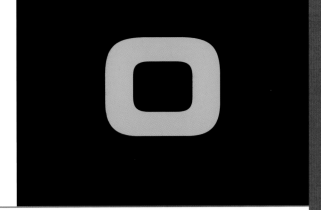

When Mike Bliss set out to run the full NASCAR NEXTEL Cup Series schedule, he did so with a great deal of racing success in other divisions before finally finding the perfect team to display his talents. When he joined team owner Gene Haas full-time in 2005, he already had many accomplishments behind the wheels of a variety of racing machines.

Bliss first began his racing career when he was only 10 years of age in go-karts around his Oregon home. Years later, he eventually competed in NASCAR's Autozone Elite Division, Northwest Series before moving to open-wheel cars. In 1993, Bliss won the USAC Silver Crown championship and in 1995 he won seven USAC sprint car races, three USAC midget races, and one Silver Crown race.

Born:	April 5, 1965, Milwaukie, Oregon
Height:	6-1
Weight:	165 lbs

Sponsor	**NetZero**
Make	**Chevrolet**
Crew Chief	**Robert "Bootie" Barker**
Team	**Haas CNC Racing**

The CNC Hass Racing Chevrolet was piloted by Mike Bliss of Milwaukie, Oregon, in 2005. Note the unique car number that works nicely with the team's primary sponsor.

NASCAR NEXTEL Cup Series Career Statistics

YEAR	RACES	WINS	TOP 5S	TOP 10S	POLES	TOTAL POINTS	FINAL STANDING	WINNINGS
1998	2	0	0	0	0	146	58th	$32,520
1999	2	0	0	0	0	104	58th	$42,475
2000	25	0	0	1	0	1748	39th	$953,948
2002	1	0	0	0	0	121	64th	$90,083
2003	1	0	0	0	0	85	65th	$65,300
2004	4	0	1	2	0	407	49th	$284,405
2005	36	0	0	2	0	3,262	28th	$3,091,108
TOTALS	71	0	1	5	0	5,783		$4,559,839

Bliss relaxes against his Chevrolet during a break and talks with his crew.

In 1998, Bliss finally made his NASCAR NEXTEL Cup Series start on September 27 at Martinsville Speedway while driving for team owner Buz McCall. Two races for Jack Birmingham in 1999 led to 24 events for him

Pit road can be a lonely place when a problem strikes. Here, Bliss comes to a stop so his car can receive some attention from his crew.

the following year. The team was eventually forced to close its doors due to a lack of sponsorship.

Bliss turned his attention to the NASCAR Craftsman Truck Series, where he won the division championship in 2002.

He kept his NASCAR NEXTEL Cup Series aspirations going, entering limited events for such legends as A. J. Foyt, Chip Ganassi, Joe Gibbs, and two events for Haas in 2004. The limited schedules simply didn't offer enough time to mold a team into a winning effort.

Bliss sports a serious look, possibly mentally preparing for an upcoming qualifying lap.

Bliss, a former **NASCAR Craftsman Truck Series** champion, feels right at home on the **NASCAR NEXTEL Cup Series.**

In 2005, Bliss was hired to drive the No. 0 Chevrolet for Haas for the entire season. One of the confidence builders came from the fact that Bliss would have Hendrick Motorsports engines under the hood, which meant added horsepower.

Highlights to his season came with a ninth-place finish at Pocono, Pennsylvania, and a seventh at Bristol, Tennessee.

Bliss hopes to someday find victory lane in NASCAR NEXTEL Cup Series competition. He realizes just how tough that goal can be to accomplish.

His closest shot at victory during the season came in the NASCAR NEXTEL All-Star Challenge, a non-points event, at Lowe's Motor Speedway in May of 2005. He was going for the victory when he and Brian Vickers tangled as they received the checkered flag. Bliss wasn't feeling very blissful when he saw Vickers get the victory.

"This is one of those nights that nothing really counts. It's a free-for-all. But I wouldn't wreck somebody for that. I would have taken second."

JEFF BURTON

31

When looking for a NASCAR NEXTEL Cup Series driver who is known as a fan favorite, one should look no further than Jeff Burton, driver of the Richard Childress Racing Chevrolet. The South Boston, Virginia, native has been a fixture within the sport over the past decade and has a enjoyed a fair amount of success on a variety of track configurations.

In 2004, Burton experienced the biggest change of his 11-year career. Due to the lack of major sponsorship on the sides and hood of the No. 99 Fords he was wheeling, Burton left the multi-car operation owned by Jack Roush in hopes of improving an uncertain future. Even though he was victorious with Roush on 17 occasions from 1997 through 2003, the chemistry that made them a consistent threat to win had slowly dissolved. It was clearly time to make a move to another racing organization.

Though he was reluctant to leave Roush, Burton found some much-needed stability with longtime championship team owner Richard Childress. The union that began for Burton and Childress in mid-August of 2004 at Michigan International Speedway is progressing steadily into a winning team of the future.

Ironically, the late Dale Earnhardt was so keen on Burton's ability to master a NASCAR race car that he wanted him as his replacement once his retirement plans were put into place.

Initially, Burton joined Childress in what was then the No. 30 car. Once Robby Gordon announced he was leaving Childress' Welcome, North Carolina–based operation, Burton was placed in the No. 31 ride Gordon had piloted, beginning with the 2005 season.

Looking back, Burton's first trip to victory lane as a NASCAR competitor came at Martinsville, Virginia, in the Busch Series in 1990, and he went on to place 15th in points that season. By 1993, the urge to go on to NASCAR NEXTEL Cup racing was simply too great to ignore. His first start came on July 11

Born: June 29, 1967, South Boston, Virginia

Height: 5-7

Weight: 155 lbs

Sponsor	**Cingular Wireless**
Make	**Chevrolet**
Crew Chief	**Kevin Hamlin**
Team	**Richard Childress Racing**

Jeff Burton, left, stands alongside fellow driver Jimmie Johnson, driver of the Hendrick Motorsports Chevrolet, in the garage area.

of that year at New Hampshire International Speedway for team owner Filbert Martocci. Burton ran well in the opening laps, but fell out after crashing on lap 86 of the 300-lap event.

Over time, Burton attracted attention from several prominent team owners, including Bill and Mickey Stavola, as well as Roush, the foundation from which all Burton's wins have come. His best season to date was 1999,

NASCAR NEXTEL Cup Series Career Statistics

YEAR	RACES	WINS	TOP 5S	TOP 10S	POLES	TOTAL POINTS	FINAL STANDING	WINNINGS
1993	1	0	0	0	0	52	---	$9,550
1994	30	0	2	3	0	2,726	24th	$594,700
1995	29	0	1	2	0	2,556	32nd	$630,770
1996	30	0	6	12	1	3,539	13th	$884,303
1997	32	3	13	18	0	4,285	4th	$2,296,614
1998	33	2	18	23	0	4,415	5th	$2,626,987
1999	34	6	18	23	0	4,733	5th	$5,725,399
2000	34	4	15	22	0	4,836	3rd	$5,959,439
2001	36	2	8	16	0	4,394	10th	$4,230,737
2002	36	0	5	14	0	4,259	12th	$4,224,856
2003	36	0	3	11	0	4,109	12th	$4,384,752
2004	36	0	2	6	0	3,902	18th	$4,054,310
2005	36	0	3	6	0	3,803	18th	$4,265,666
TOTALS	403	17	94	156	1	47,609		$39,888,083

Burton leads Mark Martin (6), Jimmie Johnson (48), and Casey Mears (41) as others fight for position behind them.

when he logged six victories, eighteen top-5s, and twenty-three top-10s. Burton posted wins that year at Charlotte; both Darlington races; Las Vegas; Rockingham, North Carolina; and the spring race at New Hampshire, where it all began.

In 2005, Burton enjoyed a third-place finish at Talladega early in the season and a strong second-place finish at Bristol Motor Speedway. But there wasn't very much more for him to get excited about, as the team struggled to find the top 10 in the finishing order.

Burton battles the 11-turn Infineon Raceway road course at Sonoma, California, in June 2005. Burton finished 30th in the race.

In 2004, Burton left team owner Jack Roush after 10 seasons to join Richard Childress and RCR Enterprises. Here is Burton in the No. 30 RCR Chevrolet.

Burton looks forward to another season with Childress in 2006, but admits he misses the victory lane celebrations he enjoyed in the past.

"Well, definitely to try to finish how we've run," Burton said. "We've been running good, we just haven't been finishing good. Somebody else has probably got into [a crash] or [there is] one we create ourselves.

"You know, our goal is still that we don't create any problems ourselves and do our best every single weekend we can and capitalize and get the finishes that we seem to think that we deserve, anyway."

During a brief break in the action, Burton confers with crewmember Gil Martin, a long time RCR employee and crew chief.

KURT BUSCH

97

If there was a driver that moved quickly into prominence, a good example would be Kurt Busch, driver of the Roush Racing Ford. His 2005 season features visits to victory lane as well as his share of adverse endings at Bristol, Tennessee; Charlotte, North Carolina; and Watkins Glen, New York.

The success story for NASCAR NEXTEL Cup Series driver Kurt Busch came about just as fast as the cars he drives in each of the 36 races on the season-long schedule. Now his resume includes the words *NASCAR NEXTEL Cup champion*, a feat he accomplished in 2004. Those are rather impressive words that greatly accent a driver's career statistics.

Busch's prestigious career came partly by chance. When team owner Jack Roush looks for new talent for his powerhouse Roush Racing NASCAR NEXTEL Cup Series organization, he does so in a very unique way. He used a *Gong Show*–style audition where drivers are invited to wheel his race cars in hopes of finding some undiscovered future superstar. The best of the

Kurt Busch, driver of the Roush Racing Ford in 2005, hustles his car to the bottom of the racetrack in hopes of gaining a position.

group gets further consideration, while the others must retreat back to the lesser-known divisions where they succeeded and excelled.

Busch proved his talents, thus gaining a position as one of Roush's current NASCAR NEXTEL Cup Series drivers. His audition, so to speak, came in the fall of 1999 when he was eventually placed in a NASCAR Craftsman Truck Series ride. The next season, Busch logged four victories in that division, which paved the way for a stellar career in the prestigious NASCAR NEXTEL Cup Series division.

Born:	August 4, 1978, Las Vegas, Nevada
Height:	5-11
Weight:	150 lbs

Sponsor	**IRWIN Industrial Tools/Sharpie**
Make	**Ford**
Crew Chief	**Jimmy Fennig**
Team	**Roush Racing**

Busch sits behind the controls of the Roush Racing Ford ready to do battle for the win.

Busch moved into NASCAR in 2000 in what was then known as the Winston Cup division. He competed in only seven events so he wouldn't upset his bid to be Rookie of the Year in 2001. He didn't win rookie honors and struggled with seven DNFs (Did Not Finish) for the season. The biggest blow of the season was his failure to qualify for the final event, then held at Atlanta Motor Speedway.

Since those early personal disappointments, Busch has consistently placed his No. 97 Ford up front and has logged a total of 13 victories in Roush's machines. In 2005, Busch visited victory lane at Phoenix, Arizona, on April 23 and Pocono, Pennsylvania, on June 12.

For the second consecutive year, Busch added his name to the list of top-10 drivers vying for the Chase for the NASCAR NEXTEL

NASCAR NEXTEL Cup Series Career Statistics

YEAR	RACES	WINS	TOP 5S	TOP 10S	POLES	TOTAL POINTS	FINAL STANDING	WINNINGS
2000	7	0	0	0	0	613	---	$311,915
2001	35	0	3	6	1	3,081	27th	$2,170,630
2002	36	4	12	20	1	4,641	3rd	$5,105,394
2003	36	4	9	14	0	4,150	11th	$5,587,384
2004	36	3	10	21	1	6,506	1st	$9,677,543
2005	34	3	9	18	0	5,974	10th	$6,516,318
TOTALS	184	14	43	79	3	24,965		$29,369,184

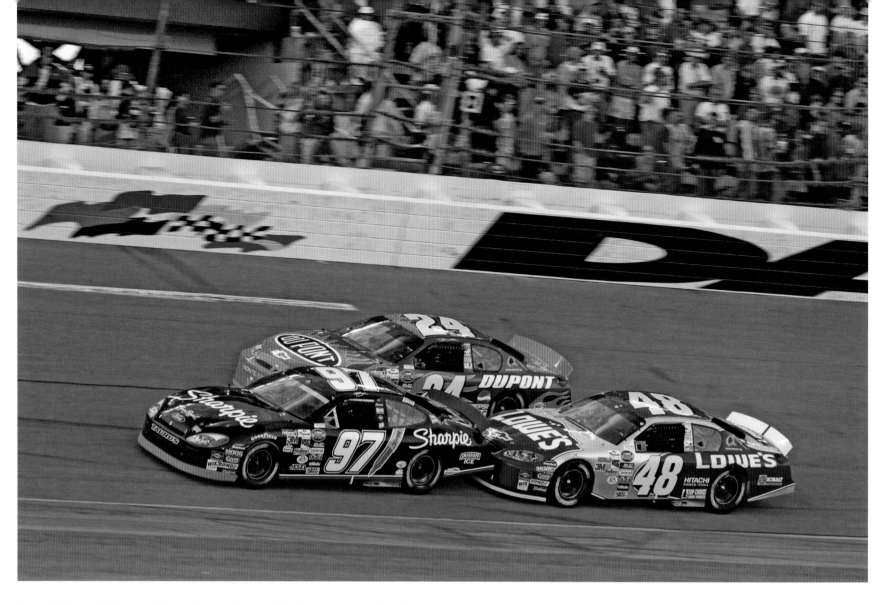

Busch (97) leads Jeff Gordon (24) and Jimmie Johnson (48) at Daytona International Speedway. He has yet to capture a win at the famed 2.5-mile track.

Busch (right) enjoys a laugh with team owner Jack Roush (center) and crew chief Jimmie Fennig while relaxing in the garage area.

Cup. Getting his second championship proved too tough an undertaking.

In a surprise move, Busch announced he would be leaving Roush Racing beginning with the 2006 NASCAR NEXTEL Cup Series season to take the Dodge vacated by Rusty Wallace, who retired from driving at the end of 2005.

Still, his mission was to make his current ride a winner while at the controls. When asked what was important until his departure, Busch said after his win at Richmond in September, "Just to be able to go out and run competitive lap times in Jack Roush's equipment. To have Jimmy Fennig lead this group it doesn't make me second-guess it, it just makes me feel good in my heart that I know that I'm getting a great effort from the crew guys and everybody behind me to go and capitalize on what's in front of us this year."

Busch gathers information from a team engineer as he sits behind the wheel of his Ford.

Sometimes that information pays off, as is the case with this victory celebration.

Busch pulls to a stop as his crew changes tires on the Roush Racing Ford. A good four-tire stop can be done in as little as 13 seconds.

Busch relaxes between one of many practice sessions.

KYLE BUSCH

5

Born: May 2, 1985, Las Vegas, Nevada

Height: 6-1

Weight: 155 lbs

Sponsor	**Kellogg's**
Make	**Chevrolet**
Crew Chief	**Alan Gustafson**
Team	**Hendrick Motorsports**

Kyle Busch, driver of the No. 5 Hendrick Motorsports Chevrolet, is finally seeing his plan to become an established driver in NASCAR's highest arena come to fruition. And from the looks of his successes, he is definitely a fast learner. In 2005, he joined a prestigious list of drivers who have won in their rookie seasons, including Dale Earnhardt, Davey Allison, Kevin Harvick, and Tony Stewart.

The younger brother of NASCAR NEXTEL Cup driver Kurt Busch, Kyle has set his sights on establishing himself quickly. Even his older brother has touted him in the past as being the best young driver to come into NASCAR NEXTEL Cup racing in a very long time.

In seven ARCA starts for Hendrick Motorsports, Kyle won twice before his 18th birthday. Of those, he won his first ARCA start at Nashville Speedway and again at Kentucky Speedway. He also scored three pole positions on the ARCA tour.

In 2001, Busch ran six NASCAR Craftsman Truck events for team owner Jack Roush as a 16-year-old high school junior, with two top-10 finishes. When he finally joined the NASCAR

Busch (left) joins team owner Rick Hendrick (center) and crew chief Alan Gustafson in victory lane at California Speedway in September 2005.

Rookie driver Kyle Busch pushes the throttle on the No. 5 Hendrick Motorsports Chevrolet.

Busch studies the job at hand while behind the wheel of his yellow and blue Chevrolet.

NASCAR NEXTEL Cup Series Career Statistics

YEAR	RACES	WINS	TOP 5S	TOP 10S	POLES	TOTAL POINTS	FINAL STANDING	WINNINGS
2004	6	0	0	0	0	345	52nd	$394,489
2005	36	2	9	13	1	3,753	20th	$4,185,239
TOTALS	42	2	9	13	1	4,098		$4,579,728

Busch (5) leads Mike Bliss (0) and Robby Gordon (7) and many others into the turn. In 2005, the 19-year-old future star made a habit of leading drivers twice his age.

Busch Series in 2003, he kept everyone on the edges of their seats by finishing second to race winner Matt Kenseth in his debut at Lowe's Motor Speedway in Charlotte, North Carolina.

In 2004, Busch ran a limited schedule of six races for team owner Rick Hendrick with his best finish being a 24th at California Speedway.

A full schedule in 2005 featured the 20-year old driver in a more confident role and much stronger equipment. He logged a second-place finish at Las Vegas, a fourth at Richmond, a second at Dover, and a fourth at Michigan.

At the event at California on September 4, 2005, he logged his first NASCAR NEXTEL Cup

Busch makes a crucial pit stop during an event at Dover International Speedway in the summer of 2005.

Busch stands before an army of photographers as he enjoys his first ever NASCAR NEXTEL Cup Series victory at Fontana, California.

Decked in a uniform adorned with sponsorship endorsements, Busch is all smiles.

victory. With the win came the honor of becoming the youngest driver to win a NASCAR event in the sport's 56-year history. Busch captured the checkered flag again at Phoenix in November.

"Being a rookie you try to find all of the edges you possibly can so you can get it out of the way. The tough races are putting yourself—either wrecking or getting loose, spinning back and doing whatever you do," Busch said at California. "It's just one of those deals where I was able to find that luck for me and it worked good enough where I was able to keep it up front."

Awaiting the start of another race, Busch positions his radio ear plugs before strapping on his helmet.

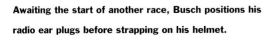

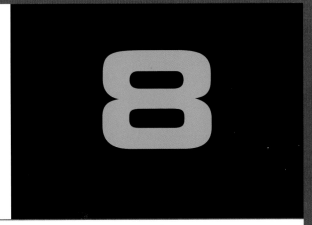

8

Throughout the 2005 NASCAR NEXTEL Cup Series season, Dale Earnhardt Jr., driver of the Dale Earnhardt, Inc. Chevrolet, would openly admit it was one of the most dismal seasons he had suffered through since first joining the NASCAR NEXTEL Cup Series circuit for five events in 1999. It was Murphy's Law in action, a testament that anything that could go wrong probably would. Earnhardt Jr. suffered through crashes, blown engines, and race after race of running well back in the pack due to handling problems within his race car's chassis. Racing up front consistently for the win had become nothing more than a distant memory.

Still, through a season of hard knocks, he enjoyed a tremendous following of fans. Ask him why he has so many fans, and he admits he's quite baffled, especially after suffering through month after month of poor finishes.

Having been on the circuit less than five years and yet to win a championship, Earnhardt Jr. shakes his head and is humbled by the thousands of fans who stand in line for hours just to see him.

When the media scouted the new faces coming into the then–Winston Cup Series during his rookie season, it came as no surprise to find the name Dale Earnhardt Jr. on their list.

In the wake of the tragic death of his father at Daytona in February 2001, Earnhardt Jr. was

Born:	October 10, 1974, Kannapolis, North Carolina
Height:	6-0
Weight:	165 lbs

Sponsor	**Budweiser**
Make	**Chevrolet**
Crew Chief	**Tony Eury Jr.**
Team	**Dale Earnhardt Incorporated**

Dale Earnhardt Jr. has made his red No. 8 famous among race fans since joining the NASCAR NEXTEL Cup Series circuit full-time in 2000.

Dale Earnhardt Jr. (8) leads Jimmy Spencer (50) during an event at Martinsville Speedway, Virginia.

looking to carry on the Earnhardt legacy in NASCAR's premier arena—without his famous father at his side offering advice and encouragement. Throughout the rest of that 2001 season, Earnhardt Jr. was the man

NASCAR NEXTEL Cup Series Career Statistics

YEAR	RACES	WINS	TOP 5S	TOP 10S	POLES	TOTAL POINTS	FINAL STANDING	WINNINGS
1999	5	0	0	1	0	500	48th	$162,095
2000	34	2	3	5	2	3,516	16th	$2,801,880
2001	36	3	9	15	2	4,460	8th	$5,827,542
2002	36	2	11	16	2	4,270	11th	$4,970,034
2003	36	2	13	21	0	4,815	3rd	$6,880,807
2004	36	6	16	21	0	6,368	5th	$8,913,510
2005	36	1	7	13	0	3,780	19th	$5,761,832
TOTALS	219	16	59	92	6	27,709		$35,317,700

Earnhardt drops the window net at the start/finish line of the Daytona International Speedway after winning the 2004 Daytona 500.

There was no question Earnhardt Jr. wanted to race just like his father. From a very young age, he followed his father's career, dreaming all the while of someday having a chance to race himself.

After a few years campaigning on the short tracks around his Mooresville, North Carolina, home, Earnhardt Jr. was ready to try out the superspeedways. He earned a NASCAR Busch Series ride with Dale Earnhardt, Inc. in 1996, and started that first event at Myrtle Beach in seventh position and finished 14th. The powerhouse started by his late father and stepmother, Teresa, in 1995 came to be a racing home for Earnhardt Jr., and he rewarded them with back-to-back NASCAR Busch Series championships, in his first year and again in 1999.

The inevitable rise to the NASCAR NEXTEL Cup Series circuit came in 1999, when Earnhardt Jr. drove in five events. The following year, he competed for Rookie-of-the-Year honors, but fell short to Matt Kenseth by a mere 42 points. When Earnhardt Jr. won his first career NASCAR Busch Series race in his 16th start, his father was there to celebrate in victory lane. And when he won his first NASCAR NEXTEL Cup race in April of 2000, his father was there, too, as a competitor. The victory celebration was one to remember. Earnhardt Jr. paid homage to his father one more time by winning the special NASCAR NEXTEL All-Star Challenge non-points event for drivers who had won races during the previous season.

Since that tragic 2001 season when he lost his father in a racing accident at Daytona, Earnhardt Jr. has logged a total of 16 victories, including six during the 2004

Earnhardt stands in the garage area and consults with crew chief Tony Eury Jr. in hopes of making the car the best it can be.

28

Earnhardt acknowledges his loyal fans at Richmond International Raceway.

Earnhardt (8) leads Elliott Sadler (38) and Kevin Harvick (29) in close quarters.

season. And even with such a horrific 2005 campaign, he managed to capture a victory at Chicago on July 10.

The victory at Chicago was a huge positive in a rather bleak season.

"Well, it couldn't have come any sooner," Earnhardt said of the win. "It gave the team a lot of confidence and a lot of morale. We had belief and we still worked hard, but this has really boosted our attitudes and our morale that we definitely needed."

Since that win, Earnhardt Jr. happily welcomed Tony Eury Jr. back into the role of crew chief at Dover, Delaware, on September 25. Many felt it was the beginning of their quest to once again run at the front. A third-place qualifying effort offered some hope, even though he ultimately finished 31st.

Earnhardt Jr. has matured into a winning race driver destined for greatness. Like his father before him, his magnificent story will simply continue to unfold.

Earnhardt showing the personality that garners him such loyal fans.

CARL EDWARDS

99

Of all the drivers to compete in NASCAR NEXTEL Cup Series in 2005, no one seemed to emerge as brightly as Carl Edwards, driver of the Roush Racing Ford. The Columbia, Missouri, native made the very best of his opportunity to wheel the ride given to him in the late stages of the 2004 NASCAR NEXTEL Cup season. He went from virtual unknown to NASCAR NEXTEL Cup Series winner in a very short amount of time.

The former substitute teacher saw his father, Mike, win more than 200 feature races while driving modified stock cars and midgets at several Midwestern tracks. That simply fueled the fire for young Carl to get involved himself, as he too was quite successful in his own right on the short tracks. His first ever race car came in the form of a Volkswagen Beetle, as he and his father were involved in a local racing division with the Edwards family operating a garage to build and service them.

That led to later becoming a two-time NASCAR Dodge Weekly Racing series champion in 1999 and 2000. Just two racing seasons later, Edwards won the 2002 Baby Grand Stock Car Association national

Born:	August 15, 1979, Columbia, Missouri
Height:	6-3
Weight:	165 lbs

Sponsor	**Office Depot**
Make	**Ford**
Crew Chief	**Bob Osborne**
Team	**Roush Racing**

Edwards poses by one of two winner's trophies he collected at Atlanta Motor Speedway.

Carl Edwards made the No. 99 Roush Racing Ford very popular in 2005, winning twice at Atlanta, and once each at Pocono and Texas.

championship, which served as another step closer to NASCAR.

Edwards then moved into the NASCAR Craftsman Truck Series, winning Rookie of the Year honors there in 2003. Also that year, Edwards finished eighth in points in the truck series and improved that mark to third in points in 2004. That was enough to convince Jack Roush that he needed to think about moving his newfound superstar to the elite NASCAR NEXTEL Cup ranks.

NASCAR NEXTEL Cup Series Career Statistics

YEAR	RACES	WINS	TOP 5S	TOP 10S	POLES	TOTAL POINTS	FINAL STANDING	WINNINGS
2004	13	0	1	5	0	1,424	37th	$1,410,570
2005	36	4	13	18	2	6,498	3rd	$4,889,993
TOTALS	49	4	14	23	2	7,922		$6,300,563

Edwards makes a pit stop late in the race at Pocono International Raceway. On the next trip to pit road, he did so as the race winner en route to victory lane.

Edwards replaced longtime Roush veteran Jeff Burton in the No. 99 machine upon Burton's departure to Richard Childress Racing in August of 2004. Edwards began compiling some strong finishes in what was then an unsponsored car. The financial backing soon came and in 13 starts, Edwards logged one top-5 and five top-10s, but the best was yet to come.

In 2005, Edwards surprised the racing world by taking his first career win at Atlanta Motor Speedway in March, beating Jimmie Johnson for the win by a half-car length. He scored his second victory at Pocono in June.

Those outings, along with a string of fourth-place finishes on the return trip to

Edwards sits ready with his helmet on, waiting for the command to start his engine.

RICHMOND

After a NASCAR Busch Series victory at Richmond International Raceway, Edwards shows off the signature back flip he performs each time he wins.

Pocono, Michigan, and Richmond, helped pave the way to the Chase for the NASCAR NEXTEL Cup. Edwards kept the back flips coming during the Chase, with back-to-back wins at Atlanta and Texas.

It was certainly a season to remember.

"I'm very fortunate," Edwards said at Richmond. "You know where I came from. This is kind of wild for me to be involved in this this early. I feel like the reason why I'm having such great success is my team. I feel like I've kind of got on board with Roush right at the crest—and Greg Biffle, all the stuff he's taught me—no, it's just unbelievable. It hasn't really set in."

Team owner Jack Roush discusses race strategy with Edwards before the start of an event.

BILL ELLIOTT

In 2005, Bill Elliott enjoyed the title of "research driver" for the second year. The title meant he would not run the entire NASCAR NEXTEL Cup Series season; rather he'd be available for the occasional race where team owner Ray Evernham wanted to try something slightly different in hopes of benefiting the championship-caliber machines

Born: October 8, 1955, Dawsonville, Georgia

Height: 6-1

Weight: 185 lbs

Sponsor	**Dodge Dealers**
Make	**Dodge**
Crew Chief	**Chris Andrews**
Team	**Ray Evernham**

NASCAR NEXTEL Cup Series Career Statistics

YEAR	RACES	WINS	TOP 5S	TOP 10S	POLES	TOTAL POINTS	FINAL STANDING	WINNINGS
1976	7	0	0	0	0	556	49th	$11,635
1977	10	0	0	2	0	1,002	36th	$20,575
1978	10	0	0	5	0	1,176	34th	$42,215
1979	14	0	1	5	0	1,709	28th	$53,215
1980	11	0	0	4	0	1,232	35th	$44,005
1981	13	0	1	7	1	1,442	31st	$70,320
1982	21	0	8	9	1	2,718	25th	$201,030
1983	30	1	12	22	0	4,279	3rd	$514,029
1984	30	3	13	24	4	4,377	3rd	$680,344
1985	28	11	16	18	11	4,191	2nd	$2,383,186
1986	29	2	8	16	4	3,844	4th	$1,049,142
1987	29	6	16	20	8	4,202	2nd	$1,559,210
1988	29	6	15	22	6	4,488	1st	$1,554,639
1989	29	3	8	14	2	3,774	6th	$899,370
1990	29	1	12	16	2	3,999	4th	$1,090,730
1991	29	1	6	12	2	3,535	11th	$705,605
1992	29	5	14	17	2	4,068	2nd	$1,692,381
1993	30	0	6	15	2	3,774	8th	$955,859
1994	31	1	6	12	1	3,617	10th	$936,779
1995	31	0	4	11	2	3,746	8th	$996,816
1996	24	0	0	6	0	2,627	30th	$716,506
1997	32	0	5	14	1	3,836	8th	$1,607,827
1998	32	0	0	5	0	3,305	18th	$1,618,421
1999	34	0	1	2	0	3,246	21st	$1,624,101
2000	32	0	3	7	0	3,267	21st	$2,580,823
2001	36	1	5	9	2	3,824	15th	$3,618,017
2002	36	2	6	13	4	4,158	13th	$4,122,699
2003	36	1	9	12	0	4,303	9th	$5,008,530
2004	6	0	0	1	0	595	38th	$567,900
2005	9	0	0	0	0	695	45th	$809,013
TOTALS	746	44	175	320	55	91,585		$37,734,922

Bill Elliott pits at the very end of pit road in California. Frequently that helps a driver get back on track the fastest.

of Kasey Kahne and Jeremy Mayfield without risking precious points.

A victory for Elliott late in the 2001 season at Homestead, Florida—the 41st win of his career—ended a six-year winless streak. When the checkered flag fell over his Ray Evernham–owned Dodge, it silenced the critics who claimed that Elliott was simply too old to find victory lane again.

But Elliott wasn't finished. In 2002, he won pole position at Pocono, Pennsylvania, and

Loudon, New Hampshire, in back-to-back efforts and continued that good fortune with a win at Pocono and the prestigious Brickyard 400 at Indianapolis Motor Speedway the next week.

Stock car racing has been all the redhead from Georgia has ever known. He and his brothers Ernie and Dan got started early, scrounging around their father's junkyard and fixing up old cars that were perfect for racing—racing around the dirt roads between junk piles, that is. The boys of George and Mildred Elliott had found their calling.

With George acting as an early sponsor and financier, the fledgling race team spent summer weekends competing on small dirt tracks. The brothers eventually persuaded their father to buy a NASCAR NEXTEL Cup Series machine, a beat-up old Ford Torino purchased from Bobby Allison. The boys first raced the car at Rockingham, North Carolina, on February 29, 1976, with Bill finishing 33rd in his debut. Still, the boys felt rich with the $640 in prize money they collected.

They struggled mightily for the next few years and threatened more than once to close the doors on the team for good. Thankfully, businessman Harry Melling entered the picture and provided the Elliotts with top-notch equipment, and the wins began to come.

The first victory finally came in the last race of the 1983 season at Riverside, California, young Elliott's 117th career start. He posted three more wins in 1984 to set the stage for an incredible 1985 season. Bill won 11 races in 28 starts, starting his assault by dominating the Daytona 500. He won at Atlanta and Darlington, and over-whelmed the competition at Talladega in May, winning the pole position with a speed of 202.398 miles per hour. He broke an oil line during the race, but made up five miles under green conditions by turning lap after lap at more than 205 miles per hour, regaining the lost deficit to win the race.

The come-from-behind victory was his second win of the four major NASCAR events. To win three meant he would be awarded a $1 million bonus from the series sponsor. Elliott suffered brake problems at the next $1 million–eligible event at Charlotte, but came back at Darlington to win the Southern 500 and the bonus in its inaugural year.

In August 1987, Elliott turned the fastest time in a stock car, reaching 212.809 miles per hour at Talladega. He was crowned NASCAR NEXTEL Cup

Elliott wheels the No. 91 Evernham Motorsports Dodge at top speed.

Lowe's Motor Speedway president H. A. "Humpy" Wheeler gets some interesting information from Elliott during a break in the action.

Elliott (91) leads Kurt Busch (97) in a NASCAR NEXTEL Cup event in 2004. Elliott campaigned a limited schedule after decades of running the full schedule.

Series champion in 1988. From 1995 to 2000, Elliott again fielded his own cars with co-owner Charles Hardy, but the two never could break into the winner's circle. When Elliott joined Evernham at the start of the 2001 season, veteran motorsports writers were predicting them to win multiple races and billed them as a dream team of sorts. The strings of multiple wins haven't come, but Elliott did prove that he is still a talented driver.

Elliott ran eight races in the 2005 season. His car was knocked out of the running by an accident early in the race in California and sidelined by engine trouble on two other occasions. His best finish was an 11th at Michigan in late August. Elliott doesn't mind his new role one bit.

"I've been blessed with a great career over the years, but this is where I want to be," Elliott says. "A limited schedule with Ray [Evernham] is perfectly fine with em. I'm really very happy with this arrangement."

Elliott's No. 91 Evernham Motorsports Dodge has become familiar to his millions of fans. It has become his number since running a limited schedule.

JEFF GORDON

24

In 2005, Jeff Gordon, driver of the No. 24 Hendrick Motorsports Chevrolet, had one mission in mind: he wanted to add another NASCAR NEXTEL Cup championship to his list of accomplishments, just as he had done in 1995, 1997, 1998, and 2001. He started off in good fashion, winning the prestigious Daytona 500, for the third time in his career.

Two more victories came at Martinsville, Virginia, on April 10 and Talladega, Alabama, on May 1. There was some promise for a fifth title, prompting Gordon himself to dub his efforts, "The Drive for Five."

Then, just as if the lights were turned off over the festive party, Gordon and his Hendrick team began a slide backward that ranks 2005 as the worst season of his 13-year career.

What possibly makes his dismal season so hard for his fans to take is he's never had a bad season. Not since "The King" Richard Petty first showed up on the NASCAR grids in 1958 has such a young driver shown, and gone on to

Jeff Gordon, driver of the Hendrick Motorsports Chevrolet, won his third Daytona 500 in 2005.

Born:	August 4, 1971, Vallejo, California
Height:	5-7
Weight:	150 lbs

Sponsor	**DuPont**
Make	**Chevrolet**
Crew Chief	**Steve Letarte**
Team	**Hendrick Motorsports**

Gordon enjoyed a special triumph at Talladega Superspeedway in May 2005. He was victorious on four occasions throughout the 2005 season.

fulfill, such overwhelming promise as Gordon. By the time he was 30 years old, he had had four NASCAR NEXTEL Cup titles under his belt—the third driver ever to win that many—and he

NASCAR NEXTEL Cup Series Career Statistics

YEAR	RACES	WINS	TOP 5S	TOP 10S	POLES	TOTAL POINTS	FINAL STANDING	WINNINGS
1992	1	0	0	0	0	70	---	$6,285
1993	30	0	7	11	1	3,447	14th	$765,168
1994	31	2	7	14	1	3,776	8th	$1,779,523
1995	31	7	17	23	8	4,614	1st	$4,347,343
1996	31	10	21	24	5	4,620	2nd	$3,428,485
1997	32	10	22	23	1	4,710	1st	$6,375,658
1998	33	13	26	28	7	5,328	1st	$9,306,584
1999	34	7	18	21	7	4,620	6th	$5,858,633
2000	34	3	11	22	3	4,361	9th	$3,001,144
2001	36	6	18	24	6	5,112	1st	$10,879,757
2002	36	3	13	20	3	4,607	4th	$4,981,170
2003	36	3	15	20	4	4,785	4th	$5,107,762
2004	36	5	16	25	6	6,490	3rd	$6,437,660
2005	36	4	8	14	2	4,174	11th	$6,855,444
TOTALS	437	73	199	269	54	60,174		$69,130,616

Gordon enjoys a victory burn-out after winning at Martinsville Speedway, Virginia, in October 2005.

Gordon gets some fast service from his Hendrick Motorsports crew just prior to returning to the track.

The multicolored DuPont designs Gordon carries on his Chevrolets have always been a fan favorite.

is widely considered the man most likely to break the record of seven championships held by Petty and Dale Earnhardt Sr. With his good looks and astounding success, Gordon has established himself as a household name to both veteran fans and schoolchildren alike.

His fans are accustomed to his successes. Each time he rolls out onto a short track or superspeedway in his familiar fluorescent and metallic blue No. 24 Chevy, he is almost expected to emerge the victor. That's why finishes like 39th at Atlanta; Richmond, Virginia; and Dover, Delaware, are not characteristic for the Vallejo, California, native.

Gordon was unable to make the 2005 Chase for the NASCAR NEXTEL Cup after some rather disappointing finishes. After the 26th event of the season at Richmond International Raceway, longtime crew chief Robbie Loomis announced he would be leaving Hendrick Motorsports at the end of the season to rejoin Petty Enterprises as vice president of competition.

That opened the door for Steve Letarte to be promoted from car chief to crew chief. Gordon then won a late-October event at

Gordon answers questions from various media outlets outside of his Hendrick Motorsports hauler.

Gordon stands quietly on pit road watching a practice session.

Gordon is always available to sign autographs for his fans.

Martinsville, offering hope for the 2006 season.

"It's disappointing (not making the Chase) but it's been a disappointing year," Gordon said after the event at Richmond. "There are so many moments throughout the year where you can look back and say 'Boy if this could of happened, we could have been in the Chase' but lately things have not gone our way and we haven't performed. It's disappointing but it's been a disappointing year and not just tonight but a lot of nights and days.

"I'm looking forward to the challenge of getting ourselves turned around and getting some excitement back in this game so we can go challenge for wins again and go out there next year."

Gordon's young-looking face can be seen as he sits behind the controls of his No. 24 Hendrick Motorsports Chevrolet.

ROBBY GORDON

7

n 2005, NASCAR NEXTEL Cup Series driver Robby Gordon experienced for the first time in his career what team ownership in NASCAR's highest arena is all about. The rewards can be tremendous when a driver and team are winning. But when wrecks and blown engines are the order of the day, maintaining a team can be rather difficult.

It's no secret that Gordon likes to race virtually anything on wheels. Like so many who began their careers in motorsports other than stock car racing, Gordon didn't grow up driving Chevrolets, Dodges, or Fords, but rather, off-road championship machines beginning in 1985.

Gordon has driven in the Indianapolis 500 on three occasions, logging respectable showings in each of those events.

Gordon joined the ranks of NASCAR in 1991 and has driven for such legendary team owners as Junie Donlavey, Robert Yates, Larry McClure, Chip Ganassi, and Richard Childress.

In November 2001, Gordon logged his first career victory at Loudon, New Hampshire, while driving in 10 events for Childress. He joined RCR Enterprises full-time in 2002 and was winless that

Robbie Gordon fielded his own cars in 2005, but suffered a variety of problems throughout the season.

first full season, but scored victories on the road courses at Sonoma, California, and Watkins Glen, New York, in 2003.

In 2004, Gordon challenged for wins from February through August but could not capture a victory. Still, there's no mistaking the competitive style he brings to the racetrack each week.

Gordon left Childress' operation on good terms, his reason being his desire to field his own operation. As he suspected, it's been a rather challenging uphill climb through the ranks in the

Born:	January 2, 1969, Cerritos, California
Height:	5-10
Weight:	180 lbs

Sponsor	**Harrah's, Jim Beam**
Make	**Chevrolet**
Crew Chief	**Greg Erwin**
Team	**Robby Gordon Motorsports**

Crew chief Greg Erwin stands alongside Gordon in the garage area.

ultra-competitive NASCAR NEXTEL Cup Series division. He failed to make the starting lineup for the season-opening Daytona 500 and has endured 10 finishes of 35th or worse. Through the event at Richmond International Raceway on September 10, he only had one top-5 and one top-10, a second one coming at Watkins Glen on August 14.

Gordon says he's in his new role of driver/team owner for the long haul.

"The next Rick Hendrick, Richard Childress, or Joe Gibbs has to come from somewhere," Gordon says. "I love the sport. I like the competition that NASCAR NEXTEL Cup gives us. The schedule is difficult. But this is something I want to do for sure. I'm 35 years old now and I believe that if we can stay on the same path, we'll be able to grow our company. We've dreamed of growing our company into something like Richard Childress has. We're working really hard and we're getting more competitive. Hopefully that becomes a reality."

NASCAR NEXTEL Cup Series Career Statistics

YEAR	RACES	WINS	TOP 5S	TOP 10S	POLES	TOTAL POINTS	FINAL STANDING	WINNINGS
1991	2	0	0	0	0	---	55th	$27,265
1993	1	0	0	0	0	---	94th	$17,665
1994	1	0	0	0	0	---	76th	$7,965
1996	3	0	0	0	1	---	57th	$32,915
1997	20	0	1	1	0	---	40th	$622,439
1998	1	0	0	0	0	---	67th	$24,765
2000	17	0	1	2	0	---	43rd	$620,781
2001	17	1	0	3	0	---	44th	$1,371,900
2002	36	0	1	5	0	---	20th	$917,020
2003	36	2	4	10	0	3,856	16th	$3,705,320
2004	36	0	2	6	0	3,646	23rd	$4,025,550
2005	29	0	1	2	0	2,117	37th	$2,276,313
TOTALS	199	3	10	29	1	9,619		$13,649,898

BOBBY HAMILTON JR.

32

Since his birth on January 8, 1978, Bobby Hamilton Jr. has known very little except the exciting world of stock car racing. But the Nashville, Tennessee, native isn't complaining. He has enjoyed a successful winning career and has now moved to NASCAR's highest arena, the NASCAR NEXTEL Cup Series.

His father, Bobby Hamilton Sr., drove short tracks around Tennessee himself for many years until given the chance to drive in NASCAR NEXTEL Cup Series competition during the making of the movie *Days of Thunder* in 1989. From there, Hamilton Sr. began a NASCAR career wherein he logged four victories.

Hamilton Sr. is now a fixture on the NASCAR Craftsman Series tour. Hamilton Jr. has followed his father into NASCAR NEXTEL Cup Series, driving for team owner Cal Wells in the No. 32 PPI Racing Chevrolet.

In 1997, Hamilton Jr.'s career began when his father bought him a 1971 Ford Pinto to race. The two quickly transformed the small compact car into a powerful racing machine that began the young star's career.

Hamilton Jr. started racing in the mini-modified division at Highland Rim Speedway near Ridgetop, Virginia. A year later, he took home a trophy as the track's season champion. He moved up the ARCA Supercar Series in 1998 and notched four top-5 finishes in just five starts.

With this father watching closely and offering advice where needed, he tested the waters of the NASCAR Busch Series in the fall of 1998 at Rockingham and Atlanta. Two years later, midway through the 2000 season, Hamilton Jr. got the opportunity to race full-time in the NASCAR Busch Series for team owner Dave Carroll.

In a surprise move in 2001, Hamilton Jr. made 10 starts in NASCAR NEXTEL Cup Series competition, seven coming with team owner Larry McClure and three with former owner Andy Petree.

Hamilton Jr. captured his first Busch Series win in 2002 at New Hampshire, setting the stage for a remarkable 2003 season. Hamilton won four times that year, at Chicago, Memphis, Kentucky, and Phoenix. He also finished fourth in the point standings while driving for Rensi Motorsports and team owners Ed Rensi, Sam Rensi, and Gary Weisbaum.

In 2004, Hamilton left the Rensi operation to take advantage of another shot at NASCAR NEXTEL Cup Series racing. During a period of re-organization within the Hickory, North Carolina–based team, driver Ricky Craven was released and some personnel were reassigned. Part of that massive change came with Hamilton Jr. being placed behind the wheel and Harold Holly being hired as crew chief.

After joining the Wells organization late in the season, Hamilton Jr. struggled with racetracks that were new to him and failed to score a top-10 finish in an abbreviated 2004 schedule.

Hamilton Jr. once again failed to crack the top 10 in the 2005 season. Despite promising runs at Atlanta, Bristol, and Dover, and a new

Born:	January 8, 1978,
	Nashville, Tennessee
Height:	5-5
Weight:	170 lbs

Sponsor	**Cal Wells**
Make	**Chevrolet**
Crew Chief	**James Ince**
Team	**PPC Motorsports**

Bobby Hamilton Jr., driver of the PPI Motorsports Chevrolet, strives to make a name for himself in NASCAR NEXTEL Cup Series competition.

crew chief in James Ince, his best finish was 11th at Las Vegas early in the season.

Hamilton Jr. knows that the NASCAR learning curve takes time.

"It's a totally different animal from the NASCAR Busch Series. Over there, you can take two or three smart people who can help you kick tail all year long. Over here, you've got to have all the pieces of the puzzle in place going in. The driver has to know everything about the racetrack and you've almost got to be in a Cup car for a couple of years to get that feel. It can be so confusing. You're constantly thinking of everything in the world, asking yourself, 'How can I pick up a second or a half-second?' It's been a real roller coaster and it's also a ton of pressure."

NASCAR NEXTEL Cup Series Career Statistics

YEAR	RACES	WINS	TOP 5S	TOP 10S	POLES	TOTAL POINTS	FINAL STANDING	WINNINGS
2004	17	0	0	0	0	1,271	39th	$1,259,210
2005	33	0	0	0	0	2,183	36th	$2,898,094
TOTALS	50	0	0	0	0	3,454		$4,157,304

KEVIN HARVICK

29

Kevin Harvick, driver of the RCR Enterprises Chevrolet, saw his share of disappointments during the 2005 NASCAR NEXTEL Cup Series season, unable to make the Chase for the NASCAR NEXTEL Cup. He did enjoy a rather convincing victory at Bristol Motor Speedway in April as a small consolation for not being able to challenge for the title.

After successful seasons in both the NASCAR Craftsman Truck Series and NASCAR Busch Series, the driver of the No. 29 RCR Enterprises Chevrolet has enjoyed a quick rise into prominence in NASCAR NEXTEL Cup Series competition. Harvick continues to compete in those NASCAR divisions whenever his schedule permits.

The death of Dale Earnhardt in 2001 escalated him to a role in NASCAR NEXTEL Cup Series competition that surprised everyone, including himself.

When the 2001 season began, Harvick was just a second-year NASCAR Busch Series driver

Born:	December 8, 1975, Bakersfield, California
Height:	5-10
Weight:	175 lbs

Sponsor	**GM Goodwrench**
Make	**Chevrolet**
Crew Chief	**Todd Berrier**
Team	**Richard Childress Racing**

Kevin Harvick, driver of the RCR Enterprises Chevrolet, proudly wears his GM Goodwrench colors.

Kevin Harvick (29) began driving the No. 29 Richard Childress Racing Chevrolet in 2001 after the death of seven-time champion Dale Earnhardt Sr.

NASCAR NEXTEL Cup Series Career Statistics

YEAR	RACES	WINS	TOP 5S	TOP 10S	POLES	TOTAL POINTS	FINAL STANDING	WINNINGS
2001	35	2	6	16	0	4,406	9th	$4,302,202
2002	35	1	5	8	1	3,501	21st	$3,748,100
2003	36	1	11	18	1	4,770	5th	$4,994,249
2004	36	0	5	14	0	4,228	14th	$4,739,010
2005	36	1	3	10	2	4,072	14th	$4,970,049
TOTALS	178	5	30	66	4	20,977		$22,753,610

for Richard Childress, a year removed from being named NASCAR Busch Series Rookie of the Year in 2000. By the end of 2001, Harvick had two cup victories, the Raybestos Rookie of the Year title, and the NASCAR Busch Series championship to his credit.

Harvick's rise was so surprising because no one could have foreseen the fate of Childress' top driver, legendary seven-time champion Earnhardt. After the black day of February 18, 2001, when Earnhardt was killed

Harvick (29) leads Bobby Labonte (18) and Tony Stewart (20) into turn one.

on the final lap of the Daytona 500, Childress turned to his new young talent to wheel his NASCAR NEXTEL Cup Series cars.

Five season have passed since Harvick first made his presence known in NASCAR's most coveted form of racing. He recorded wins at Atlanta and Chicago in 2001, another win at Chicago in 2002, Indianapolis in 2003, and a win in the 2005 season at Bristol, Tennessee, on April 3.

As far as his 2005 statistics, his season was one of both good and not-so-good finishes. Either he would finish in the top 10 or his car number would be listed toward the end of the

Harvick enjoys one of his many NASCAR Busch Series victories. He is a former champion in the NASCAR Busch Series.

Harvick gets some advice from 1989 NASCAR NEXTEL Cup Series champion Rusty Wallace.

Harvick lifts a unique trophy given to him for winning at Bristol Motor Speedway in April 2005. It was his first NASCAR NEXTEL Cup Series victory at the track.

Harvick smiles as he helps the crew push his car to pit road for qualifying.

race results. The strength was there when they were on their game, but when he and his team were off, Harvick admits some mistakes hurt their efforts. The team is working to find that missing consistency needed to run up front.

Still, they could look to the win at Bristol as their highest point of the season.

"You have to learn how to get out of a hole," Harvick said after his win at Bristol. "I think that's one thing that RCR has always been really good at, recovering from being down. And they always come back stronger than what they were before."

The silver and black colors of Harvick's Chevrolet have become a familiar sight around the NASCAR tracks over the past few seasons.

DALE JARRETT

88

T hroughout the 2005 NASCAR NEXTEL Cup Series season, Dale Jarrett, driver of the Robert Yates Racing Ford, continued to hold onto his championship hopes even when they looked rather grim toward the cut-off point at Richmond in September. As in 2004, consistent top-5 finishes eluded him for much of the season, but with only a couple of months to go to complete the season, a top-10 berth into the new Chase for the NASCAR NEXTEL Cup program wasn't out of the question.

Even though he didn't make it into the Chase, the highlight of his season came on

Dale Jarrett leads Rusty Wallace (2) on the concrete surface of Martinsville (VA) Speedway.

Born: November 26, 1956, Conover, North Carolina
Height: 6-2
Weight: 215 lbs

Sponsor	**UPS**
Make	**Ford**
Crew Chief	**Todd Parrott**
Team	**Robert Yates Racing**

Jarrett relaxes while dressed in the brown-and-yellow colors of UPS, his primary sponsor.

October 2, when he returned to victory lane at Talladega Superspeedway after a two-year absence from winning races. The best part of the equation included being reunited with crew chief Todd Parrott just one week before the victory. The two had been together in 1999 when Jarrett won the NASCAR NEXTEL Cup Series championship.

Jarrett became championship material early

NASCAR NEXTEL Cup Series Career Statistics

YEAR	RACES	WINS	TOP 5S	TOP 10S	POLES	TOTAL POINTS	FINAL STANDING	WINNINGS
1984	3	0	0	0	0	267	---	$7,345
1986	1	0	0	0	0	76	---	$990
1987	24	0	0	2	0	2,177	25th	$143,405
1988	29	0	0	1	0	2,622	23rd	$118,640
1989	29	0	2	5	0	2,789	24th	$232,317
1990	24	0	1	7	0	2,558	25th	$214,495
1991	29	1	3	8	0	3,124	17th	$444,256
1992	29	0	2	8	0	3,251	19th	$418,648
1993	30	1	13	18	0	4,000	4th	$1,242,394
1994	30	1	4	9	0	3,298	16th	$881,754
1995	31	1	9	14	1	3,584	13th	$1,363,158
1996	31	4	17	21	2	4,568	3rd	$2,985,418
1997	32	7	20	23	3	4,696	2nd	$3,240,542
1998	33	3	19	22	2	4,619	3rd	$4,019,657
1999	34	4	24	29	0	5,262	1st	$6,649,596
2000	34	2	15	24	3	4,684	4th	$5,984,475
2001	36	4	12	19	4	4,612	5th	$5,366,242
2002	36	2	10	18	1	4,415	9th	$3,935,670
2003	36	1	1	7	0	3,358	26th	$4,055,487
2004	36	0	6	14	0	4,214	15th	$4,539,330
2005	36	1	4	7	1	3,960	15th	$4,705,436
TOTALS	603	32	162	256	17	72,134		$50,549,255

Dale Jarrett (88) battles for position with Matt Kenseth (17) at Lowe's Motor Speedway in October 2005.

on by learning his never-give-up attitude from his famous father, Ned Jarrett, a two-time NASCAR NEXTEL Cup champion in his own right, who taught young Dale that the journey could be long and hard and unpredictable.

The list of teams Jarrett has driven for reads as a who's who list of prominent, legendary NASCAR teams owners. Former driver Cale Yarborough, the Wood Brothers, Joe Gibbs, and Robert Yates have all given the longtime NASCAR star the necessary equipment to win races and championships. All totaled, Jarrett has collected 31 NASCAR victories since joining the tour full-time in 1989.

As a result of those triumphs, a championship was awarded to him while driving

Jarrett sits among a few tools in the garage area as he watches his crew turn wrenches on his car.

Jarrett (88) leads teammate Elliott Sadler (38) as Kasey Kahne (9), Terry Labonte (44), and Mike Wallace (4) trail behind.

for Robert Yates, the first for Jarrett as well as for the longtime team owner. Since that once elusive title was scored, his position in the point standings has steadily dropped.

In 2000, Jarrett was fourth in points, fifth in 2001, ninth in 2002, twenty-sixth in 2003, and back to fifteenth in 2004. In 2005, Jarrett and his Bill Wilburn–led crew missed making the Chase for the NASCAR NEXTEL Cup elite.

As with many other drivers in 2005, Jarrett and Co. searched for consistency within their program. His best finishes of the season came with a fifth at Bristol, Tennessee, on April 3, a ninth at Talladega, Alabama, on May 1, an eighth at Charlotte on May 29; and back-to-back fifth-place finishes at Sonoma, California; and Daytona Beach, Florida, on June 26 and July 2, respectively.

Leading up to the win, Jarrett posted a number of top-15 finishes through the 36-race schedule. That's especially impressive considering the fact Jarrett lost his original crew chief, Mike Ford, who

resigned for personal reasons in early summer.

Through the Chase-deciding event at Richmond International Raceway on September 10, Jarrett had gone winless in the first 26 races. His last win prior to Talladega came on February 23, 2003, at the North Carolina Motor Speedway, a track no longer being used in NASCAR competition.

Jarrett still thinks of that memorable Rockingham victory.

"I'm not sure that I treated the one at Rockingham special enough," Jarrett said after his win at Talladega. "We were so used to winning in those days that I didn't see any reason that we wouldn't continue on winning races, at least a couple a year. That was what we were used to doing. Our program got to the point that we weren't in a position to do that much, so that's what makes this so special and this one will be treated a lot more special.

"I think that we do have more victories to go. I think in the next two years to come that we can visit

victory lane a number of times, but in case that doesn't happen, we're gonna make sure that we enjoy this one. All of these have been very special. I can go back and talk about each and every one of them [and] something that made each one of them special, but today came at a very good time for a lot of us—for Todd and myself, and for Robert and Doug [Yates], and especially for everyone at UPS."

Jarrett gets crucial fresh tires and gas from the UPS pit crew.

JIMMIE JOHNSON

48

When Jimmie Johnson looks back at the 2005 NASCAR NEXTEL Cup Series season, he most likely will do so with all of the positives in mind.

He and his Hendrick Motorsports team did win races, enough to make some teams consider it an awesome season. Their definition of *awesome* would require the label of *champion* tacked on to the season-long highlights shown in New York at the NASCAR Awards banquet.

Johnson and his team did secure a solid place among those in the Chase for the NASCAR NEXTEL Cup. The string of top-10 finishes they enjoyed during the first half of the season simply didn't materialize as much during the 10 events of the Chase. Still, with fellow Hendrick Motorsports drivers Jeff

Born: September 17, 1975, El Cajon, California
Height: 5-11
Weight: 175 lbs

Sponsor	**Lowe's Home Improvement**
Make	**Chevrolet**
Crew Chief	**Chad Knaus**
Team	**Hendrick Motorsports**

Jimmie Johnson's No. 48 Hendrick Motorsports Chevrolet has become a fixture in victory lane since the team was formed in 2001.

Johnson peeks out from behind his helmet as he prepares to exit his Hendrick Motorsports Chevrolet.

Gordon, Brian Vickers, and Kyle Busch not eligible to battle for the championship, it was all up to Johnson and crew chief Chad Knaus to carry the Hendrick banner.

The El Cajon, California, native has since logged 18 victories, including wins in 2005 at Las Vegas in March, Charlotte in May, and Dover in September. It's no surprise he established himself early as one of the top drivers to lock himself into the Chase of 2005, leading the point standings for the majority of the events.

Johnson suffered his worst finish of the season at Indianapolis in the Brickyard 400 in August where he finished 38th in the 43-car field after a late-race crash. Further, Johnson and his team missed their opportunity to qualify for the race at Indianapolis, were forced to start the race from the rear, and weren't able to recover.

NASCAR NEXTEL Cup Series Career Statistics

YEAR	RACES	WINS	TOP 5S	TOP 10S	POLES	TOTAL POINTS	FINAL STANDING	WINNINGS
2001	3	0	0	0	0	213	---	$122,320
2002	36	3	6	21	5	4,600	5th	$2,847,700
2003	36	3	14	20	2	4,932	2nd	$5,517,850
2004	36	8	20	23	1	6,498	2nd	$5,692,620
2005	36	4	13	22	1	6,406	5th	$6,976,664
TOTALS	147	18	53	86	9	22,649		$21,157,154

Johnson gets left-side service from his crew during a crucial pit stop. His Chad Knaus–led Hendrick Motorsports crew is known for getting off of pit road in record time.

Some teams would have been derailed by such terrible results, but not Johnson's. They are championship contenders, and the next step in the plan is to find the missing consistency that had propelled them to greatness in season's past.

Johnson realizes his remarkable fortune, having such good equipment under him week to week. It seems to show best each time he fires his engine at Lowe's Motor Speedway, located just a mile from the Hendrick Motorsports facility. He is the only driver in history to win three consecutive Coca-Cola 600s, coming in 2003, 2004, and 2005.

Kyle Busch (left) joins Johnson as they watch Johnson's crew work on his car in the garage area.

Team owner Rick Hendrick (center) stands in victory lane at Charlotte with Johnson (left) and crew chief Chad Knaus as race winners. Seeing them there has become a familiar sight.

Johnson, like Gordon, enjoys those victory burn-outs.

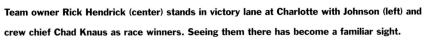

Jeff Gordon (left), Johnson's co–team owner and teammate, joins him in the garage area.

"There's a lot of people who have been in the sport who have watched Rick and his family through the years before I was able to get in here and start driving for him. I watched from a distance and always dreamed of driving for the team," Johnson says. "To be able to be here and be a part of it, there isn't anywhere else I would want to be. I can't tell you how blessed and thankful I am to be a part of this team."

Johnson is the only driver to win three consecutive Coca-Cola 600s at Lowe's Motor Speedway.

KASEY KAHNE

9

Born: April 10, 1980, Enumclaw, Washington

Height: 5-7

Weight: 130 lbs

Sponsor	**Dodge**
Make	**Dodge**
Crew Chief	**Tommy Baldwin Jr.**
Team	**Evernham Motorsports**

Throughout the 2005 NASCAR NEXTEL Cup Series season, Kasey Kahne was considered one of the drivers with the most potential to win races. After all, his rookie season of 2004 was clearly behind him and he had been readily accepted by his fellow drivers. Plus, he had the engine strength and equipment of Evernham Motorsports under him.

The predicted string of wins didn't come, but he did manage to produce some strong top-10 finishes including one victory at Richmond in May.

Kahne is relatively quiet in nature, often speaking in a monotone voice even after spending the previous four hours at speeds over 200 miles per hour.

Instead, he would rather make his statements from the lead position, and he has placed his solid-red Dodge in position to win in many of the 36 races that make up the schedule.

Kahne has four-time NASCAR champion Jeff Gordon to thank for his good fortune. Like Kahne, Gordon was a superstar within the sprint-car ranks before being discovered by

team owner Rick Hendrick. Kahne's ability to wheel one of those same open-wheel machines led Ray Evernham, Gordon's former crew chief, to give him a shot at NASCAR NEXTEL Cup Series racing in one of his Dodges. Evernham knew he had found a diamond the rough.

After two years of driving in the NASCAR Busch series full-time, Kahne rewarded his faithful team owner by winning the 2004 NASCAR Rookie-of-the-Year honors.

Today, Kahne, driver of the No. 9 Evernham Motorsports Dodge, is a rising star within the NASCAR arena. In his first season, Kahne had 13 top-5 finishes and 14 top-10s, including four second-place finishes.

The highlights of Kahne's 2005 season came in the form of that elusive first victory at Richmond, as well as a strong second-place finish in the prestigious Brickyard 400 at Indianapolis Motor Speedway. Kahne also logged a fifth at Atlanta, a third and Darlington, South Carolina, and a two sixth-place finishes at New Hampshire and California as some of his best finishes of the season.

Kahne recently signed a contract extension to drive for Evernham for many more years, making them a championship-contending team of the future.

"Ray and the Evernham Motorsports organization are committed to building a championship team," Kahne said. "The personnel and resources are in place to achieve that objective. This long-term agreement reflects the confidence we have in our commitment to succeed, to win races and compete for championships.

"I'm really looking forward to the future with Evernham Motorsports and the No. 9 Dodge Dealers/UAW Dodge Charger. I think great things are in store for us in the near future."

Kahne often sports his sunglasses when relaxing around the racetrack.

Kahne leads the field at Indianapolis Motor Speedway in August 2005.

Kasey Kahne has made the No. 9 a winning number in 2005.

NASCAR NEXTEL Cup Series Career Statistics

YEAR	RACES	WINS	TOP 5S	TOP 10S	POLES	TOTAL POINTS	FINAL STANDING	WINNINGS
2004	36	0	13	14	4	4,274	13th	$4,759,020
2005	36	1	5	8	2	3,611	23rd	$4,874,838
TOTALS	72	1	18	22	6	7,885		$9,633,858

MATT KENSETH

17

For the second consecutive year of NASCAR's Chase for the NEXTEL Cup, Matt Kenseth, driver of the Roush Racing Ford, enjoyed being a part of it. But in 2005, he had to rally with some impressive finishes to gain his invitation into the championship hunt. A win at Bristol Motor Speedway on August 27 certainly paved the way to gain one of 10 positions in the Chase.

Kenseth is used to championship pressure. He won the 2003 NASCAR championship in such a convincing manner that some insiders feel his dominant championship performance may have prompted NASCAR officials to change the format.

The Madison, Wisconsin, native gained the points lead in March 2003 after his win at Las Vegas and held it for the remainder of the 36-race season. Further, he did so with numbers so far ahead of the second-place finisher that he would have had to sit out several races for anyone to have caught up.

Kenseth's driving career began when his father bought a race car and had his son maintain it with a few friends who helped on the crew. Once Matt reached his 16th birthday, his dad gave him the car. He progressed to the ARTGO Series (now NASCAR Auto Zone Elite Division) and became its youngest winner (besting NASCAR driver Mark Martin for that honor).

Kenseth's Roush Racing crew makes changes to the No. 17 Ford in hopes of better chassis performance.

A large part of getting into NASCAR's biggest arena is getting noticed. Kenseth was hired by Jack Roush for the full 2000 NASCAR NEXTEL Cup Series season after five races with Roush in 1999. The young driver shocked the racing community by winning the Coca-Cola 600 at Lowe's Motor Speedway in May that year. His 14th-place finish in the points standings was good enough to bring Kenseth the Rookie of the Year award in 2000.

After a winless 2001 campaign, Kenseth quickly asserted himself at the front of the pack in 2002. He claimed victory at Rockingham, North Carolina, in the second race of the season,

Born: March 10, 1972, Madison, Wisconsin

Height: 5-9

Weight: 152 lbs

Sponsor	**DeWalt Tools**
Make	**Ford**
Crew Chief	**Robbie Reiser**
Team	**Roush Racing**

captured another checkered flag at Texas Motor Speedway in April, and added a third trophy to the shelf with a win at Michigan in June. Kenseth also scored victories at Richmond, Virginia, in September and Phoenix, Arizona, in November to become the winningest driver of the season.

The 2004 NASCAR NEXTEL Cup Series season proved to be a bit more of a challenge in respect to wins, as he collected two wins early in the season at Rockingham, North Carolina, and Las Vegas. Still, Kenseth was consistently in the top 10 in the NASCAR NEXTEL Cup Series standings.

In 2005, Kenseth endured his problems throughout the season, as well as during a few events in the final 10 events of the season. Still, the fact that he was all but out of the Chase and came back to gain a spot is a victory in itself.

"To gain points and have a great day, that can happen with the equipment that we have and all the stuff that we have, but to have five or six people have trouble and have a great day for several weeks in a row is a difficult task," Kenseth says. "We've been a lot more competitive, I think, since around June. There have certainly been some races that we haven't been competitive and we messed things up, but on average we've been much more competitive.

"We just have awesome engines and we have great cars and if we can do the right things to them and not mess them up, they can run like that."

NASCAR NEXTEL Cup Series Career Statistics

YEAR	RACES	WINS	TOP 5S	TOP 10S	POLES	TOTAL POINTS	FINAL STANDING	WINNINGS
1998	1	0	0	1	0	150	---	$42,340
1999	5	0	1	1	0	434	29th	$143,561
2000	34	1	4	11	0	3,711	14th	$2,408,138
2001	36	0	4	9	0	3,982	13th	$2,565,579
2002	36	5	11	19	1	4,432	8th	$3,888,850
2003	36	1	11	25	0	5,022	1st	$4,038,124
2004	36	2	8	16	0	6,069	8th	$6,223,890
2005	36	1	12	17	2	6,352	7th	$5,781,774
TOTALS	220	10	51	99	3	30,152		$25,092,256

TRAVIS KVAPIL

77

Travis Kvapil most certainly knows the meaning of good fortune. It's the way he feels each time he roams through the massive race shops of Penske Racing in Mooresville, North Carolina, where his race cars are housed and maintained throughout the NASCAR NEXTEL Cup Series racing schedule of events.

With that massive, state-of-the-art facility comes a name that is a champion in a variety of auto racing ventures. That name belongs to Roger Penske, a longtime team owner in NASCAR competition dating back to the early 1970s with such drivers as Dave Marcis, the late Mark Donohue, and Bobby Allison.

Kvapil now finds himself as one of those drivers Penske has tapped as a star of the future. That's music to a driver's ears, considering the fact Kvapil now has the best equipment that money can buy under him. In order to continue seeing his name edged on the rooflines of a fleet of yellow Dodges that sit shiny and ready to race, he must perform well. He must win races. He must also someday win a championship. There's a good chance the

wins and titles will come for the Janesville, Wisconsin, native.

Kvapil's credentials include being named the 2001 NASCAR Craftsman Truck Rookie of the Year, the 2003 Craftsman Truck Series champion, and the winner of Toyota's first victory in that series in 2004 at Michigan.

When it comes to his NASCAR NEXTEL Cup Series efforts, Kvapil is still learning. His only top-10 through Talladega in October of 2005 was a seventh at Bristol Motor Speedway in April. His next best performances were two 17th-place finishes at Dover and Pocono in June.

Kvapil is still optimistic he will soon begin logging top-10s and top-5s enroute to someday scoring that elusive first win.

Born:	March 1, 1976, Janesville, Wisconsin
Height:	6-0
Weight:	170 lbs

Sponsor	**Kodak**
Make	**Dodge**
Crew Chief	**Shane Wilson**
Team	**Penske-Jasper Racing**

Travis Kvapil takes the No. 77 Penske Racing Dodge through its paces during the 2005 season.

Kvapil feels comfortable as a full-time fixture in the NASCAR NEXTEL Cup Series.

NASCAR NEXTEL Cup Series Career Statistics

YEAR	RACES	WINS	TOP 5S	TOP 10S	POLES	TOTAL POINTS	FINAL STANDING	WINNINGS
2004	3	0	0	0	0	213	63rd	$171,475
2005	36	0	0	2	0	3,077	33rd	$3,288,454
TOTALS	39	0	0	2	0	3,290		$3,459,929

"Competing in NASCAR NEXTEL Cup Series competition is tougher than any other racing division anywhere," Kvapil says. "It's a manner of learning all you can and getting as much track time as possible. Hopefully we'll start getting better finishes. We just have to keep working hard."

BOBBY LABONTE

18

Born: May 8, 1964, Corpus Christi, Texas

Height: 5-9

Weight: 175 lbs

Sponsor **Interstate Batteries**
Make **Chevrolet**
Crew Chief **Steve Addington**
Team **Joe Gibbs Racing**

Yes, there have been weeks in 2005 when the Corpus Christi, Texas, native shined brightly. His best race of the year came at Charlotte, North Carolina, in May when he lost the race to Jimmie Johnson by a fender. Add to that a sixth-place finish at Phoenix, an eighth at Richmond, and a third at New Hampshire, and one can see there have been some bright spots for Labonte to dwell upon in 2005.

It's finishes like 43rd at Daytona, 40th at Indianapolis, and 38th at Texas, to name only a few, that have kept Labonte and his team from finding the consistency to challenge for the win each week. It's been a slow process trying to turn those dismal finishes into top-15s, top-10s, top-5s, and finally, the victories that he is so used to delivering. His last visit to victory lane came on November 16, 2003, at Homestead-Miami Speedway.

Labonte's crew chief Michael McSwain left the team in July of 2004. Brandon Thomas filled in for the remainder of the year and was replaced by Steve Addington at the beginning of 2005. Still, the struggles continue.

From all he's accomplished, it seems that Labonte was born to be a stock car racer. Back in 1984, a shy and rather young Bobby could be found over and underneath the Chevrolets that his older brother Terry would drive. That year, the elder Labonte captured his first NASCAR NEXTEL Cup Series championship. While Terry was accepting the trophy and all the checks, Bobby's mental wheels began turning toward putting his own racing career in motion.

After several years of winning on the short tracks, Labonte began his NASCAR Busch Series career in 1990. The next year, he came back to win the NASCAR Busch Series championship. By 1993, he found a home with Bill Davis Racing but lost Raybestos Rookie of - the Year honors to future NASCAR NEXTEL Cup Series champion Jeff Gordon. Having finished 19th and 21st in the point standings in his first two full seasons, Labonte was happy to take the ride with Joe Gibbs Racing when Dale Jarrett vacated the spot to join Robert Yates in 1995.

Five years later, he joined brother Terry on the list of NASCAR champions. All of his 21 career victories and 26 pole positions have come while with Gibbs. But as of the past two seasons, Labonte has gone winless and endured his share of struggles and heartache. Labonte only finished in the top-10 six times. The 2005 season was his last with the team

"It's been rather anguishing. It's been frustrating," Labonte said in *NASCAR Illustrated*. "We definitely didn't want it to turn out this way and didn't start the season off like we wanted to. We've had some struggles with performance. We've struggled with things happening that shouldn't have happened. If we had had some better performances, it would have off-set some of it."

NASCAR NEXTEL Cup Series Career Statistics

YEAR	RACES	WINS	TOP 5S	TOP 10S	POLES	TOTAL POINTS	FINAL STANDING	WINNINGS
1992	2	0	0	0	0	110	---	$8,350
1993	30	0	0	6	1	3,221	19th	$395,660
1994	31	0	1	2	0	3,038	21st	$550,305
1995	31	3	7	14	2	3,718	10th	$1,413,682
1996	31	1	5	14	4	3,590	11th	$1,475,196
1997	32	1	9	18	3	4,101	7th	$2,217,999
1998	33	2	11	18	3	4,180	6th	$2,980,052
1999	34	5	23	26	5	5,061	2nd	$4,763,615
2000	34	4	19	24	2	5,130	1st	$7,361,386
2001	36	2	9	20	1	4,561	6th	$4,786,779
2002	36	1	5	7	0	3,810	16th	$3,851,770
2003	36	2	12	17	4	4,377	8th	$4,745,258
2004	36	0	5	11	1	4,277	12th	$4,570,540
2005	36	0	4	7	0	3,488	24th	$4,627,404
TOTALS	438	21	110	184	26	52,662		$43,747,999

Labonte enjoyed a great deal of success with team owner Joe Gibbs, including the 2000 NASCAR NEXTEL Cup championship.

TERRY LABONTE

44

As the 2005 NASCAR NEXTEL Cup Series Series season began, Terry Labonte, driver of the Hendrick Motorsports Chevrolet, had a brand new driving plan in mind. For the first time in his 27-year career, he would run a limited schedule for both the 2005 and 2006 seasons. Then, once his 2006 obligations were complete, he would retire from driving. It was a good way to gradually step away as opposed to having to exit his cars in one last, sad farewell.

Born: November 16, 1956, Corpus Christi, Texas

Height: 5-10

Weight: 165 lbs

Sponsor	**Kellogg's**
Make	**Chevrolet**
Crew Chief	**Mike Ford**
Team	**Hendrick Motorsports**

NASCAR NEXTEL Cup Series Career Statistics

YEAR	RACES	WINS	TOP 5S	TOP 10S	POLES	TOTAL POINTS	FINAL STANDING	WINNINGS
1978	5	0	1	3	0	659	39th	$20,545
1979	31	0	2	13	0	3,615	10th	$130,057
1980	31	1	6	16	0	3,766	8th	$215,889
1981	31	0	8	17	2	4,052	4th	$334,987
1982	30	0	17	21	2	4,211	3rd	$363,970
1983	30	1	11	20	3	4,004	5th	$362,790
1984	30	2	17	24	2	4,508	1st	$713,010
1985	28	1	8	17	4	3,683	7th	$694,510
1986	29	1	5	10	1	3,473	12th	$522,235
1987	29	1	13	22	4	4,002	3rd	$825,369
1988	29	1	11	18	1	4,007	4th	$950,781
1989	29	2	9	11	0	3,564	10th	$704,806
1990	29	0	4	9	0	3,371	15th	$450,230
1991	29	0	1	7	1	3,024	18th	$348,898
1992	29	0	4	16	0	3,674	8th	$600,381
1993	30	0	0	10	0	3,280	18th	$531,717
1994	31	3	6	14	0	3,876	7th	$1,125,921
1995	31	3	14	17	1	4,146	6th	$1,558,659
1996	31	2	21	24	4	4,657	1st	$4,030,648
1997	32	1	8	20	0	4,177	6th	$2,270,144
1998	33	1	5	15	0	3,901	9th	$2,054,163
1999	34	1	1	7	0	3,580	12th	$2,475,365
2000	32	0	3	6	1	3,433	17th	$2,239,716
2001	36	0	1	3	0	3,280	23rd	$3,011,901
2002	36	0	1	4	0	3,417	24th	$3,143,990
2003	36	1	4	9	1	4,162	10th	$3,643,695
2004	36	0	0	6	0	3,519	26th	$3,745,240
2005	14	0	0	1	0	1,071	40th	$1,202,520
TOTALS	831	22	181	360	27	100,112		$38,272.137

Terry Labonte (44) passes younger brother Bobby (18) at Bristol Motor Speedway.

The two-time NASCAR NEXTEL CUP champion has performed on a variety of track configurations, but he would admit his career of late has been on his terms, giving him extended time away from the track. It's something he's never been able to enjoy prior to the 2005 season. The full schedule he's been running for over two decades has been quite time consuming.

Labonte's career began when team owner Billy Hagan picked him to drive his NASCAR cars when Terry was only 22 years old and working as a crew member for him. The two eventually won the 1984 NASCAR NEXTEL Cup championship together just five years after joining forces.

Two years later, Labonte joined team owner Junior Johnson, collecting four victories before leaving to join Richard Jackson in 1990.

Another stint with Hagan from 1991 through 1993 proved winless, but it did set the

Labonte pulls in for a pit stop during an event at California Speedway. The race was a part of a limited 2005 schedule for the Texas native.

through 1993 proved winless, but it did set the stage for some of Labonte's best years. While struggling to take his car into the top-10 in the fall event at North Wilkesboro, North Carolina, powerhouse team owner Rick Hendrick noticed Labonte. Seeing Labonte's determination, he offered him the ride that was being vacated by Ricky Rudd, a surprise move that turned Labonte's career around.

The union between Hendrick and Labonte began with the 1994 season and produced a total of 12 victories through the 2004 season. The

Labonte brothers Terry (left) and Bobby sport their colorful drivers' uniforms. Both are past NASCAR NEXTEL CUP champions.

biggest prize, however, came in 1996 when Labonte won his second career championship, just barely edging out teammate Jeff Gordon for the title.

Labonte collected more victories with Hendrick than any other car owner he's driven for. Of those, one of his biggest came in the prestigious Southern 500 at Darlington Raceway on August 31, 2003. His win in the 1980 Southern 500 22 years earlier helped launch his career and prompted prominent team owners to take notice of him.

When Labonte approached Hendrick about the idea to heavily curtail his schedule, it happened to come at the perfect time. Hendrick had been grooming 19-year old Kyle Busch for a NASCAR NEXTEL Cup Series Series ride and the departure would allow Busch to drive Labonte's No. 5 machine and Labonte to wheel the No. 44. Since the number was Labonte's first championship number as well as the number used for his first win in 1980, Kyle Petty, the driver holding the number at Petty Enterprises, graciously allowed him to use it for 2005 and 2006.

An unexpected twist came during the 2005 season. Labonte was offered a chance to wheel the No. 11 Joe Gibbs Racing Chevrolet in select events while also continuing for Hendrick. Although involved in a limited schedule, he's shown he can still produce stellar finishes. He logged twelfth-place finishes at both Pocono, Pennsylvania, and

Crew chief Mike Ford (left) makes some critical chassis notations as Labonte looks on. The two have enjoyed several top-10 finishes together.

Sonoma, California, and also collected a ninth-place finish at Richmond in September.

Labonte is quick to say he's enjoying his present schedule very much.

"Well, it's been different for sure," Labonte said in *NASCAR Illustrated*. "After going to all the races for 25 years and not missing one, it felt kind of strange to sit at home and watch a couple of them on TV. It felt real strange, actually. But I adjusted to it rather quickly. I've just been kind of goofing off and doing a bunch of different things. And I've been fishing some. I went down to Florida for a while. There are a lot of days I'm not sure what I'll do that day."

Labonte delivered the pizza for a few events in 2005.

Labonte sits quietly as he studies activities in the garage area.

STERLING MARLIN

O f all the drivers in NASCAR NEXTEL Cup Series Series racing, none are more down to earth than Sterling Marlin, a farm boy turned racer who had the dream to be a racer just as his father did before him. Sadly, Marlin lost his father and hero, Clifton "Coo Coo" Marlin, in August of 2005.

Born: June 30, 1957, Columbia, Tennessee

Height: 6-0

Weight: 180 lbs

Sponsor	**Coors Light**
Make	**Dodge**
Crew Chief	**Steve Boyer**
Team	**Chip Ganassi Racing**

NASCAR NEXTEL Cup Series Series Career Statistics

YEAR	RACES	WINS	TOP 5S	TOP 10S	POLES	TOTAL POINTS	FINAL STANDING	WINNINGS
1976	1	0	0	0	0	76	---	$565
1978	2	0	0	1	0	226	---	$10,170
1979	1	0	0	0	0	123	---	$505
1980	5	0	0	2	0	588	42nd	$29,810
1981	2	0	0	0	0	164	---	$1,955
1982	1	0	0	0	0	94	---	$4,015
1983	30	0	0	1	0	2,980	19th	$143,564
1984	14	0	0	2	0	1,207	37th	$54,355
1985	8	0	0	0	0	721	37th	$31,155
1986	10	0	2	4	0	989	36th	$113,070
1987	29	0	4	8	0	3,386	11th	$306,412
1988	29	0	6	13	0	3,621	10th	$521,464
1989	29	0	4	13	0	3,422	12th	$473,267
1990	29	0	5	10	0	3,387	14th	$369,167
1991	29	0	7	16	2	3,839	7th	$633,690
1992	29	0	6	13	5	3,603	10th	$649,048
1993	30	0	1	8	0	3,355	15th	$628,835
1994	31	1	5	11	1	3,443	14th	$1,127,683
1995	31	3	9	22	1	4,361	4th	$2,253,502
1996	31	2	5	10	0	3,682	8th	$1,588,425
1997	32	0	2	6	0	2,954	25th	$1,301,370
1998	32	0	0	6	0	3,530	13th	$1,350,161
1999	34	0	2	5	1	3,397	16th	$1,797,416
2000	34	0	1	7	0	3,363	19th	$1,992,301
2001	36	2	12	20	1	4,741	3rd	$4,517,634
2002	29	2	8	14	2	3,703	18th	$3,711,150
2003	36	0	0	11	0	3,745	18th	$3,960,809
2004	36	0	3	7	0	3,857	21st	$4,117,750
2005	35	0	1	5	0	3,183	30th	$4,080,118
TOTALS	675	10	83	215	13	75,740		$35,769,366

Marlin drives the silver Coors Light Dodge for Chip Ganassi Racing.

Now, after nearly three decades of racing in NASCAR, Marlin, driver of the Chip Ganassi Racing Dodge, has never let fame and success taint his easygoing country personality.

The sound of race engines roaring and welders crackling has filled Marlin's ears for as long as he can remember. Throughout Sterling's formative years, there was always some kind of stock car in the shed out back.

At the age of 15, Marlin helped on his dad's pit crew during the summer, and the underage driver occasionally took the wheel of the transporter on the long trips from Columbia, Tennessee, to places like Michigan, Daytona, or Texas. When school was in session, Marlin worked on his dad's cars but stayed home to play football.

Marlin's Chip Ganassi Racing crew changes tires and adds fuel during a race at Atlanta Motor Speedway in spring 2004.

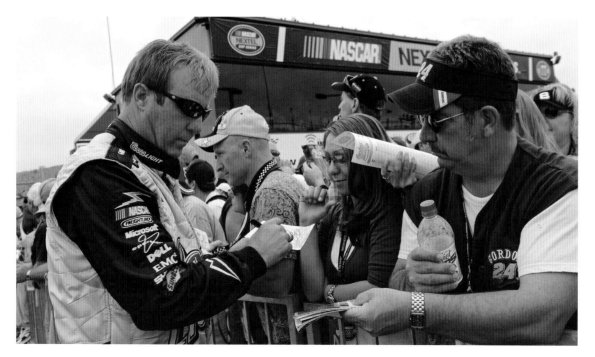

Marlin soon got the chance to fulfill his dream of driving stock cars. With help from his father's Winston Cup sponsor, H. B. Cunningham, the 16-year-old Marlin purchased a 1966 Chevelle to race at the Nashville Speedway. Soon after, in only his third start in a race car, Marlin relieved his father in a NASCAR Winston Cup event at Nashville on July 17, 1976. He finished eighth. A year later, he joined his father for his first superspeedway race, running an ARCA (Automobile Racing Club of America) car at Talladega.

Marlin continued on the short tracks and won three consecutive track championships at

Marlin always enjoys meeting the fans and signing autographs.

Jamie McMurray (left) talks with Marlin, his 2005 teammate at Chip Ganassi Racing.

Marlin (40) edges ahead of Scott Riggs (10) at Richmond International Raceway.

Marlin (40) leads Travis Kvapil (77), Dale Earnhardt Jr. (8), and Jimmie Johnson (48) as they battle for position on the track.

Morgan-McClure Racing and later with Chip Ganassi.

After nearly 300 starts and nine second-place finishes, Marlin earned his first Cup victory at the 1994 Daytona 500. He defended his Daytona 500 crown the following year, making him only the third driver in history to claim back-to-back Daytona 500 triumphs. Four more victories followed with McClure in 1995 and 1996: two at Talladega, one at Darlington, and a July win at Daytona.

After four winless seasons, Marlin rebounded with new team owner Ganassi in 2001, capturing two checkered flags and the third-place spot in the final points standings. The 2002 campaign started off well, with Marlin taking, and holding, the top spot in the point standings for 25 events on the schedule. He solidified his lead with victories at Las Vegas and Darlington in March, and by finishing in the top 10 in eight of the first ten races. A potentially serious neck injury sidelined him for the final seven events. Still, he remained optimistic.

Marlin returned in 2003 but went winless. More of the same followed for both 2004 and 2005. Due in part to the fact he has not been victorious in over three seasons, Marlin has parted ways with Ganassi for the 2006 season, joining MB2 Motorsports and team owners Nelson Bowers and Jay Frye.

"This is a great opportunity for me and I'm real excited," Marlin said. "Plus I get to run No. 14, my Dad's number."

the Nashville Speedway in 1980, 1981, and 1982. He campaigned the full NASCAR NEXTEL Cup Series schedule in 1983 and went on to win Raybestos Rookie of the Year honors driving for Roger Hamby.

Marlin struggled with various team owners until 1986, when he joined Billy Hagan for four full seasons. Two more seasons with Junior Johnson and one with Stavola Brothers Racing set the stage for his greatest successes, with

MARK MARTIN

6

Mark Martin, driver of the Roush Racing Ford, admits openly that he's at a crossroads with his NASCAR NEXTEL Cup Series Series career. There were definite plans to retire from NASCAR's elite division, but he has now elected to give the NASCAR NEXTEL Cup Series Series season one more shot. Many indications place Martin in the No. 6 Ford for one more season, even though that wasn't his original plan. He also plans to continue to field a truck in the NASCAR Craftsman Truck Series.

Jamie McMurray, the driver of the Chip Ganassi Racing Dodge in 2005, is set to replace Martin once he leaves the confines of NEXTEL Cup. Ganassi has McMurray locked into his contract for one more year, thus, prompting Martin to remain in his ride for one more year.

In 2005, Martin enjoyed runs good enough to give him a place among the 10 drivers in the Chase for the NEXTEL Cup. Martin was victorious at Kansas on Oct. 9 and won the special non-points NEXTEL All-Star event at Lowe's Motor Speedway.

Born:	January 9, 1959, Batesville, Arkansas
Height:	5-6
Weight:	135 lbs

Sponsor	**Pfizer/Viagra**
Make	**Ford**
Crew Chief	**Pat Tryson**
Team	**Roush Racing**

Mark Martin stands alongside of his Roush Racing Ford. He has driven car No. 6 for the past 17 years.

NASCAR NEXTEL Cup Series Series Career Statistics

YEAR	RACES	WINS	TOP 5S	TOP 10S	POLES	TOTAL POINTS	FINAL STANDING	WINNINGS
1981	5	0	1	2	2	615	42nd	$13,950
1982	30	0	2	8	0	3,181	14th	$126,655
1983	16	0	1	3	0	1,621	30th	$99,655
1986	5	0	0	0	0	488	48th	$20,515
1987	1	0	0	0	0	46	---	$3,550
1988	29	0	3	10	1	3,142	15th	$223,630
1989	29	1	14	18	6	4,053	3rd	$1,019,250
1990	29	3	16	23	3	4,404	2nd	$1,302,958
1991	29	1	14	17	5	3,914	6th	$1,039,991
1992	29	2	10	17	1	3,887	6th	$1,000,571
1993	30	5	12	19	5	4,150	3rd	$1,657,622
1994	31	2	15	20	1	4,250	2nd	$1,628,906
1995	31	4	13	22	4	4,320	4th	$1,893,519
1996	31	0	14	23	4	4,278	5th	$1,887,396
1997	32	4	16	24	3	4,681	3rd	$2,532,484
1998	33	7	22	26	3	4,964	2nd	$4,309,006
1999	34	2	19	26	1	4,943	3rd	$3,509,744
2000	34	1	13	20	0	4,410	8th	$3,098,874
2001	36	0	3	15	2	4,095	12th	$3,797,006
2002	36	1	12	22	0	4,762	2nd	$5,279,400
2003	36	0	5	10	0	3,769	17th	$4,048,847
2004	36	1	10	15	0	6,399	4th	$3,948,500
2005	36	1	12	19	0	6,428	4th	$5,994,353
TOTALS	638	35	227	359	41	86,800		$48,436,382

Martin is a realist and realizes just how hard winning a NASCAR NEXTEL Cup Series Series event can be. The competition gets tougher with each passing season, and more drivers and teams have the money and talent to win races.

Still, Martin finds a way to meet that challenge, as he has finished in the top 5 in the point standings on 10 occasions and the top 10 in points 15 times.

As a result of numerous short track championships around his Batesville, Arkansas, home, Martin took his winning ways

Roush Racing's No. 6 Ford has had Mark Martin's name associated with it since he joined team owner Jack Roush in 1988. Here, he is seen racing at Martinsville (VA) Speedway.

to the NASCAR NEXTEL Cup Series arena in 1981, using a couple of his own cars to battle the best stock car drivers in the world. He scored two pole positions that year, one top-5, and one top-10. The strong start grabbed the attention of more than one team owner, but Martin again fielded his own team for the full schedule in 1982. He came up short to Geoff Bodine in the Rookie of the Year race, and fell short to the bank for the many dollars spent. His only chance to survive was to drive for someone with a much larger bank account than his.

Team owner J. D. Stacy hired Martin in 1983, but the relationship didn't last. To Martin's

Martin holds the checkered flag after winning the special non-points NASCAR NEXTEL All-Star Challenge at Charlotte in May 2005.

Martin (6) holds his position, with Jimmie Johnson (48) close on his bumper.

Martin pits his car with a paint scheme that resembles one of his past machines.

Martin is definitely a fan favorite. Here he speeds past a packed grandstand of stock car racing fans.

22, 1989, at North Carolina Motor Speedway in Rockingham. Since then, Martin and Roush have scored 33 more victories and 41 pole positions. Together they have built a powerhouse organization that now features five teams in NASCAR NEXTEL Cup Series competition with fellow drivers Greg Biffle, Kurt Busch, Carl Edwards, and Matt Kenseth. All five made it into the Chase in 2005.

At age 46, Martin was still showing he has what it takes to get the job done. So much so that he had a solid, legitimate chance to win his first career NASCAR NEXTEL Cup Series championship in 2005.

"This is exactly the kind of season I had hoped and dreamed for," Martin says. "Not only has the Cup thing been very, very stellar, aside from some bad luck, but we've won a couple of Busch races, and we've won an IROC [International Race of Champions] race. This is what I was looking for, but as you know, most of what I've looked for in this business I haven't gotten, I've only gotten part of it.

"It's an honor and a privilege to drive for these [Roush] guys, and my biggest fear would be to have less of a team or less of a car to work with, but thanks to Pat [Tryson-crew chief] and thanks to Jack Roush, here we are."

surprise, as well as that of the motorsports media, he was fired after only seven races. Martin picked up rides where he could over the next four years until he interviewed Jack Roush, automotive engineer set to form a NASCAR NEXTEL Cup Series Series team in 1987. The two joined forces at the beginning of the 1988 season with their first victory coming on October

JEREMY MAYFIELD

19

Jeremy Mayfield, driver of the Evernham Motorsports Dodge, is the quiet type, and slipped into the 2005 Chase for the NEXTEL Cup virtually unnoticed. As long as the driver gets there, words are unnecessary; it's the end result that counts.

Mayfield is from Owensboro, Kentucky, a place known as an unofficial racing capital of sorts, since several very successful NASCAR stars have come from there. His has been a rather long and unpredictable road toward stardom, but for the second year in a row, he was a contender for the championship.

Mayfield didn't begin honing his stock car racing talents until 1993 when he joined the ARCA ranks full-time after spending several years driving go-karts, Street Stocks, Sportsman, and Late Models. Winning the 1987 Rookie of the Year award at Kentucky Motor Speedway certainly helped pave the way to bigger and better things.

Jeremy Mayfield put the No. 19 Evernham Motorsports Dodge in victory lane in 2004. His solid-red machine is known for its lime-green frontal tape and top number, distinguishing it from the No. 9 driven by teammate Kasey Kahne.

Born:	May 27, 1969, Owensboro, Kentucky
Height:	6-0
Weight:	190 lbs

Sponsor	**Dodge Dealers**
Make	**Dodge**
Crew Chief	**Richard "Slugger" Labbe**
Team	**Evernham Motorsports**

Mayfield displays the winner's trophy after a victory at Chicago in July 2005.

Mayfield turned to team owner Earl Sadler to help him finally make his NASCAR NEXTEL Cup debut at Charlotte in October 1993. Sadler had fielded cars for several notable up-and-coming drivers—including the late Davey

NASCAR NEXTEL Cup Series Career Statistics

YEAR	RACES	WINS	TOP 5S	TOP 10S	POLES	TOTAL POINTS	FINAL STANDING	WINNINGS
1993	1	0	0	0	0	76	---	$4,830
1994	20	0	0	0	0	1,673	37th	$226,265
1995	27	0	0	1	0	2,637	31st	$436,805
1996	30	0	2	2	1	2,721	26th	$592,853
1997	32	0	3	8	0	3,547	13th	$1,067,203
1998	33	1	12	16	1	4,157	7th	$2,332,034
1999	34	0	5	12	0	3,743	11th	$2,125,227
2000	32	2	6	12	4	3,307	24th	$2,169,251
2001	28	0	5	7	0	2,651	35th	$2,682,603
2002	36	0	2	4	0	3,309	26th	$2,494,580
2003	36	0	4	12	1	3,736	19th	$2,962,228
2004	36	1	5	13	2	6,000	10th	$3,892,570
2005	36	1	4	9	0	6,073	9th	$4,566,913
TOTALS	381	5	48	96	9	43,630		$25,553,362

Mayfield stands atop of his Ray Evernham Motorsports Dodge after his victory at Chicago. It was his only victory of the 2005 NASCAR NEXTEL Cup Series season.

Allison—so Mayfield appeared to be on the right path. He wheeled Sadler cars for four races in 1994, and T. W. Taylor also brought Mayfield on for four events that year. Then NASCAR legend Cale Yarborough called and asked for Mayfield's services. Many predicted it would be a prosperous marriage, but after 12 races in 1994 and a full season in 1995, the wins simply didn't come.

Late in the 1996 season, owners Yarborough and Michael Kranefuss swapped drivers. Mayfield went to work for Kranefuss, while John Andretti went over to Yarborough's

Behind the controls of his Evernham Motorsports Dodge, Mayfield is waiting to fire his engine.

Mayfield crosses the start/finish line at Chicago.

Mayfield gets service from his crew, something that occurs at breakneck speed hundreds of times during any given season.

Mayfield can often be seen as intense or can be seen relaxing behind a pair of sunglasses while waiting for race action to begin.

team. (Andretti won the 400-mile event at Daytona for Yarborough in 1997.)

After Kranefuss joined forces with racing legend Roger Penske, Mayfield had the best ride of his career. He scored wins at Pocono, Pennsylvania, in 1998 and 2000, as well as a win at California in 2000. In addition, there were pole positions at Darlington, Dover, Rockingham, Talladega, and Texas.

Despite the two wins, not all was well in 2000, as things slowly unraveled for the Penske-Mayfield partnership. When Mayfield's car was found to be too low after the California win, it seemed to mark the beginning of the

end. Even though Mayfield had nothing to do with the height of the car, there was discord within the team. Finally, after someone put an additive in his gas tank just before Mayfield's pole position run at Talladega, the end was all but written.

Apparently, both owner and driver wanted and needed a change after the tumultuous 2000 campaign. Mayfield finally got his wish the day after the inaugural event at Kansas Speedway in September 2001, when Penske Racing released Mayfield from his contract.

At the start of the 2002 season, Mayfield joined Ray Evernham, but went winless that

season as well as in 2003. In 2004, however, Mayfield won the Richmond event in September, and that win propelled him to the Chase for the NEXTEL Cup. The race proved he could win when it counted most.

In 2005, Mayfield logged some consistent finishes, won at Michigan and made his way into the spotlight in stellar fashion.

"It feels good to get back in the Chase," Mayfield said at Richmond. "I'm really proud of these guys. They gave me good stuff all year. We just keep getting better and better. I'm just real proud of them and real happy and glad to be back in the Chase two years in a row."

JAMIE McMURRAY

Of all the new hot drivers who have come to NASCAR NEXTEL Cup Series racing over the past few years, Jamie McMurray, driver of the Chip Gannassi Racing Dodge, is considered a champion in the making. Just ask team owner Jack Roush, who has already signed him to a contract beginning in 2006. McMurrray has certainly risen to prominence quickly.

McMurray's last win came in late 2002 and proved that Cinderella finishes can unfold and dreams really do come true. Of the millions of fans and the close-knit NASCAR fraternity witnessing the conclusion of the 500-mile event at Lowe's Motor Speedway on October 13, McMurray was probably the most surprised of them all at the outcome.

To set the stage, veteran driver Sterling Marlin was injured in a crash at Kansas on September 29, 2002, and couldn't compete for the rest of the season, after leading the point standings for 25 consecutive weeks. Team owner Chip Ganassi had had his eye on McMurray as a possible third team driver in

Born:	June 3, 1976, Joplin, Missouri
Height:	5-9
Weight:	150 lbs

Sponsor	**Havoline**
Make	**Dodge**
Crew Chief	**Donnie Wingo**
Team	**Chip Ganassi Racing**

Jamie McMurray wheels the No. 42 Chip Ganassi Racing Dodge around the road course at Sonoma, California.

McMurray seems to be enjoying his place in the sun as he's dressed in his black-and-red Havoline team colors.

2003 but had not yet presented him with a contract. McMurray's win at Charlotte while substituting for Marlin confirmed Ganassis's intuition.

McMurray continued to look for that elusive second victory, even though he has logged a number of NASCAR Busch Series wins.

In 2005, McMurray, under the direction of crew chief Donnie Wingo, posted a fourth-place

NASCAR NEXTEL Cup Series Career Statistics

YEAR	RACES	WINS	TOP 5S	TOP 10S	POLES	TOTAL POINTS	FINAL STANDING	WINNINGS
2003	36	0	5	13	1	3,965	13th	$2,699,969
2004	36	0	9	23	0	4,597	11th	$3,676,310
2005	36	0	4	10	1	4,130	12th	$3,923,968
TOTALS	108	0	18	46	2	12,692		$10,300,247

McMurray comes to a stop on pit road while his crew "rebuilds" his car with new tires and a full tank of fuel.

finish at Las Vegas, a second at Texas, a fifth at Talladgea, a sixth at Darlington, a second at Daytona, and an eighth at California, totalling four top-5s and six top-10s through Talladega in October. The rest, unfortunately have been less desirable finishes.

Whether with Ganassi or Roush in 2006, McMurray is no doubt cut from championship material and is expected to someday join that coveted list. Add to that his flair and personality, and one can see why he has become a public relations dream.

When asked about his 2005 season, it was clear that McMurray feels there have been

McMurray waits patiently inside his Chip Ganassi–owned Dodge. He is one of stock car racing's newest stars.

McMurray is a crowd favorite each time he comes to the racetrack, often getting cheers from his supporters.

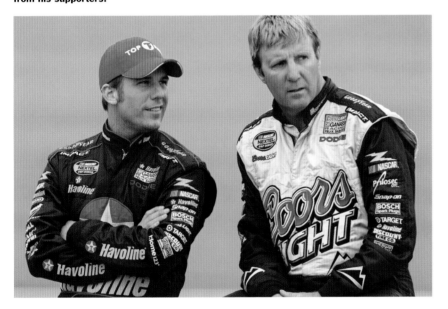

McMurray (left) talks with Sterling Marlin, his 2005 teammate at Chip Ganassi Racing.

McMurray listens intently as he receives information about his car.

reasons to celebrate as well as reasons to work harder to find the win that seems at times far away.

"It's been OK. We haven't been near as consistent this year as we were last year," McMurray said of his 2005 season in *NASCAR Illustrated*. "Some of that comes from luck. But we just haven't hit on it every week. They [NASCAR] changed some of the tires and spoilers and we just haven't caught on as well as some of the other teams."

McMurray (42) leads Terry Labonte (44), Sterling Marlin (40), and Ryan Newman (12) as they battle for the lead.

CASEY MEARS

41

Born: March 12, 1978, Bakersfield, California

Height: 5-8

Weight: 158 lbs

Sponsor	**Target**
Make	**Dodge**
Crew Chief	**Jimmy Elledge**
Team	**Chip Ganassi Racing**

The name Mears is about as familiar to auto racing as the names Woods and Palmer are to professional golf. With that in mind, auto racing enthusiasts may recognize the name Casey Mears, driver of the Chip Ganassi Racing Dodge, since he is the nephew of Rick Mears, a four-time winner of the Indianapolis 500. He is also the son of two-time Indianapolis 500 starter and off-road legend Roger Mears.

In 2005, young Casey didn't visit victory lane as he had hoped, but he did produce a few respectable finishes in his red-and-white Ganassi Racing Dodge. A seventh-place finish at Las Vegas, a fourth at Texas, a ninth at Chicago, and sixth at Indianapolis were the highlights to a season that featured many double-digit finishes.

Mears followed an interesting path toward NASCAR NEXTEL Cup Series racing. The younger Mears stuck with the family's tradition by winning his first feature event at Mesa Marin in 1994 at the mere age of 16. From there, young Casey put together impressive numbers.

Casey Mears, the nephew of Indy car great Rick Mears, is trying to make his mark as a stock car driver. Here, he peaks out from behind the shield of his helmet.

Casey Mears takes his No. 41 Ganassi Racing Dodge to its limits. His Dodge carries one of the more unique paint schemes.

He won the 1995 Jim Russell USAC Triple Crown championship at age 17 and followed that with three races of off-road competition in the SuperLites in 1996. In 1999, he finished second in the Indy Lights Series and became only the fourth driver in series history to complete every lap.

By 2000, the speeds were getting quite a bit higher. Mears successfully completed his rookie test for the Indianapolis 500 that year. He also finished third in the Indy Lights Series,

NASCAR NEXTEL Cup Series Career Statistics

YEAR	RACES	WINS	TOP 5S	TOP 10S	POLES	TOTAL POINTS	FINAL STANDING	WINNINGS
2003	36	0	0	0	0	2,638	35th	$2,639,178
2004	36	0	1	9	2	3,690	22nd	$3,250,320
2005	36	0	3	9	0	3,637	22nd	$4,234,171
TOTALS	108	0	4	18	2	9,965		$10,123,669

Casey Mears makes a pit stop for tires and fuel from Jimmy Elledge–led crew. Often times, races are won or lost on pit road.

scoring his first win at the Grand Prix of Houston by the end of 2000.

Stock cars were slowly making their way into the picture. Mears finished ninth in an ARCA event in 2001, and by the following year had a full-time ride in the NASCAR Busch Series, where he produced two top-10s in 34 starts. In December of that year, he announced he would drive for team owner Chip Ganassi in NASCAR's highest division for the entire 2003 season.

Casey Mears (left), crew chief Jimmy Elledge (center), and team manager Tony Glover look on from the garage area.

Ryan Newman (12) battles with Mears (41) with slightly damaged machines during a short track event at Martinsville Speedway, Virginia.

No wins came to the young star, but he did manage to gain quite a bit of experience racing against the likes of fellow teammates Jamie McMurray and Sterling Marlin, as well as an entire cast of NASCAR stars.

No wins have come to Mears after three seasons, but it's not due to a lack of effort on his part or the part of his crew.

"We've worked hard to get a win but so far, it hasn't come," Mears says. "We've been close a few times. We've just got to keep working hard and take it a step at a time."

Mears sits behind the wheel of his Chip Ganassi Racing–owned Dodge, waiting for the command to fire his engine.

JOE NEMECHECK

01

Each time Joe Nemechek slides into the MB2 Motorsports Chevrolet, he does so with an admirable mission in mind. With our country presently at war, Nemechek would love nothing more than to win races to boost the morale of those fighting to keep our country free.

From an early age, Nemechek has never been one to do things in a haphazard manner. He won Rookie-of-the-Year honors and championships in three straight years: the Mini Stock series in 1987, Late Model Series in 1988, and the NASCAR All-Pro Series in 1989. He went on to take the NASCAR Busch Series championship in 1992 before officially joining the NASCAR NEXTEL Cup Series ranks in 1993. To date, he is a four-time winner in NASCAR NEXTEL Cup competition and has collected over $16 million in career earnings.

Nemechek has driven for some of the most respected teams in the business, namely, Felix Sabates, Andy Petree, Rick Hendrick, and Travis Carter.

Joe Nemechek (01) leads Scott Wimmer (22) as they head into Turn 1.

Since joining his current team owner, Tom Beard, in 2003, he has moved even closer to making the art of winning commonplace.

Born: September 26, 1963, Lakeland, Florida

Height: 5-9

Weight: 185 lbs

Sponsor	**US Army**
Make	**Chevrolet**
Crew Chief	**Ryan Pemberton**
Team	**MB2 Motorsports**

Nemechek has four career wins to his credit. He first win came in the second event at New Hampshire International Speedway while with Sabates, and was followed with a win at North Carolina Motor Speedway in 2001 for Petree. In 2003, Hendrick enjoyed a victory from Nemechek at Richmond International Raceway. His last win to date came at Kansas Speedway in October 2004.

In 2005, he logged several finishes outside of the top 10. But the end result wasn't a true testament of how the Lakeland, Florida, native has performed on the racetrack.

A tenth at Martinsville in April, along with another tenth at Phoenix, a third at Pocono at Michigan, a ninth at Watkins Glen, and an eighth again at Michigan certainly gave him something to smile about.

Nemechek is ready to add more wins to his tally sheet. His Ryan Pemberton–led crew has produced some rather strong machines that have routinely gotten Nemechek to the front. Bad luck and accidents not of his making plagued him at times in 2005.

He is ready for his luck to change.

"Our finishes haven't shown how good we've run," Nemechek says. "So we need to just get to where we're finishing the races like we've been running. But we've had a few mechanical problems and it's knocked us back a little bit."

NASCAR NEXTEL Cup Series Career Statistics

YEAR	RACES	WINS	TOP 5S	TOP 10S	POLES	TOTAL POINTS	FINAL STANDING	WINNINGS
1993	5	0	0	0	0	389	44th	$56,580
1994	29	0	1	3	0	2,673	27th	$389,565
1995	29	0	1	4	0	2,742	28th	$428,925
1996	29	0	0	2	0	2,391	34th	$666,247
1997	30	0	0	3	2	2,754	28th	$732,194
1998	32	0	1	4	0	2,897	26th	$1,343,991
1999	34	1	1	3	3	2,956	30th	$1,634,946
2000	34	0	3	9	1	3,534	15th	$2,105,042
2001	31	1	1	4	0	2,994	28th	$2,510,723
2002	33	0	3	3	0	2,682	34th	$2,453,020
2003	36	1	2	6	0	3,426	25th	$2,560,484
2004	36	1	3	9	2	3,878	19th	$3,872,410
2005	36	0	2	9	1	3,953	16th	$4,223,376
TOTALS	394	4	18	59	9	37,269		$22,977,503

RYAN NEWMAN

12

Born: December 8, 1977, South Bend, Indiana

Height: 5-11

Weight: 207 lbs

Sponsor	**ALLTEL**
Make	**Ford**
Crew Chief	**Matt Borland**
Team	**Penske Racing**

When it comes to talking about the 2005 NASCAR NEXTEL Cup Series season, Ryan Newman, driver of the Penske Racing Dodge, is counting his blessings. After a rather tense race at Richmond on September 10, he was able to secure a spot in the Chase for the NEXTEL Cup. But it took some hard work, perfect strategy, and a few nail-biting moments before the spot was finally his. Even though he didn't win to get in, like Jeremy Mayfield did in 2004, having a place in the Chase felt just as good or better than going to victory lane. That was his win of the night.

Newman has often brought his mathematical equations into play on the racetrack. After all, he's a graduate of Purdue University with a degree in engineering. His entire game plan was to use that knowledge to make his race cars perform better in hopes of scoring more victories. What he learned has

Ryan Newman, driver of the No. 12 Penske Racing Dodge, leads Greg Biffle in the Roush Racing Ford as they fight for track position under green flag conditions.

Newman raises his winner's trophy high after taking the victory at New Hampshire International Speedway in September 2005.

come in handy, especially in his NASCAR NEXTEL Cup Series career.

Like Kasey Kahne, Newman has Jeff Gordon to thank for his NASCAR career. His open-wheel sprint car experience prompted

NASCAR NEXTEL Cup Series Career Statistics

YEAR	RACES	WINS	TOP 5S	TOP 10S	POLES	TOTAL POINTS	FINAL STANDING	WINNINGS
2000	1	0	0	0	0	40	---	$37,825
2001	7	0	2	2	1	652	49th	$465,276
2002	36	1	14	22	6	4593	6th	$4,373,830
2003	36	8	17	22	11	4711	6th	$4,827,377
2004	36	2	11	14	9	6,180	7th	$5,152,670
2005	36	1	8	16	8	6,359	6th	$5,578,114
TOTALS	152	12	52	76	35	22,535		$20,435,092

Ryan Newman enjoys the lead at New Hampshire International Raceway.

team owners Roger Penske, Don Miller, and Rusty Wallace to look on the dirt tracks of the Midwest. The result was the discovery of Newman, a 24-year-old open-wheel star who was already in the Quarter Midget Hall of Fame.

He pulled off wins in ARCA competition at Pocono, Kentucky Speedway, and Charlotte. He was also victorious in all three USAC divisions: Midgets, Sprint Cars, and the Silver Bullet Series.

Being named to Penske's organization carried a huge amount of clout, as Penske is known around the world in several forms of auto racing for having the best equipment and

Newman (left) enjoys a laugh with four-time NASCAR NEXTEL Cup Series champion Jeff Gordon.

Newman (12) finds himself in close quarters with Johnny Sauter (09), followed by several fellow competitors.

Newman's Penske Racing Dodge is serviced in the last pit stall on pit road. It is often reserved for the pole position winner, an honor Newman has enjoyed many times during his brief career.

Newman's eyes show his eagerness to get strapped into his race car for the job at hand.

talent that money can buy. Having the endorsement of Wallace, the 1989 NASCAR NEXTEL Cup Series champion, made acceptance in the garage area a bit easier. From there, Newman would slowly gain their respect on and off the racetrack.

Since winning his first pole position in only his third NASCAR start on May 24, 2001, the 2002 Raybestos NASCAR Rookie of the Year has made a habit of winning pole positions and has collected

35 since that first lightning-fast run at Charlotte.

His first victory came on September 15, 2002, at Loudon, New Hampshire. Even though weather dictated NASCAR's decision to red-flag the event in its late stages, the win was still was credited to Newman in the record books.

Since that first win, Newman has visited victory lane on 11 more occasions, including a victory at New Hampshire International Speedway on September 19, 2005. It was

the only victory for the No. 12 Dodge in the 2005 schedule.

Newman feels there have been many positives in his 2005 season to dwell upon.

"I think we've learned a lot about our ALLTEL Dodge, but, I think we can do, definitely, a lot better than we have," Newman says. "We ran really good at Charlotte, and we struggled at Atlanta and Texas. Like I said, we've made some big gains, and we'll see if they pay off."

KYLE PETTY

45

There were two missions for Kyle Petty in 2005. One was to work toward getting Petty Enterprises back to winning form. The other was to continue building something very close to the hearts of the Petty family: the Victory Junction Gang Camp for children suffering from disease. The camp was built in honor of Kyle's late son, Adam Petty, who lost his life during a practice session at Loudon, New Hampshire, in May of 2000.

First, he wanted to return luster to the team that has the most wins in all of NASCAR history. That's 268 to be exact, including 200 from his father, Richard Petty; 54 from his

Born: June 2, 1960, Trinity, North Carolina

Height: 6-2

Weight: 195 lbs

Sponsor	**Georgia-Pacific**
Make	**Dodge**
Crew Chief	**Paul Andrews**
Team	**Petty Enterprises**

NASCAR NEXTEL Cup Series Career Statistics

YEAR	RACES	WINS	TOP 5S	TOP 10S	POLES	TOTAL POINTS	FINAL STANDING	WINNINGS
1979	5	0	0	1	0	559	37th	$10,810
1980	15	0	0	6	0	1,690	28th	$36,350
1981	31	0	1	10	0	3,335	12th	$112,289
1982	29	0	2	4	0	3,024	15th	$120,730
1983	30	0	0	2	0	3,261	13th	$157,820
1984	30	0	1	6	0	3,159	16th	$324,555
1985	28	0	7	12	0	3,523	9th	$296,367
1986	29	1	4	14	0	3,537	10th	$403,242
1987	29	1	6	14	0	3,732	7th	$544,437
1988	29	0	2	8	0	3,296	13th	$377,092
1989	19	0	1	5	0	2,099	30th	$177,022
1990	29	1	2	14	2	3,501	11th	$746,326
1991	18	1	2	4	2	2,078	31st	$413,727
1992	29	2	9	17	3	3,945	5th	$1,107,063
1993	30	1	9	15	1	3,860	5th	$914,662
1994	31	0	2	7	0	3,339	15th	$806,332
1995	30	1	1	5	0	2,638	30th	$698,875
1996	28	0	0	2	0	2,696	27th	$689,041
1997	32	0	2	9	0	3,455	15th	$984,314
1998	33	0	0	2	0	2,675	30th	$1,287,731
1999	32	0	0	9	0	3,103	26th	$1,278,953
2000	19	0	0	1	0	1,441	41st	$894,911
2001	24	0	0	0	0	1,673	43rd	$1,008,919
2002	36	0	0	1	0	3,501	42nd	$1,995,820
2003	33	0	0	0	0	2,414	37th	$2,293,222
2004	35	0	0	0	0	2,811	33rd	$2,780,130
2005	36	0	0	2	0	3,288	27th	$3,465,687
TOTALS	749	8	51	170	8	77,633		$23,926,427

Kyle Petty (45) drives through the garage exit at Pocono International Raceway.

grandfather, Lee Petty; and 14 more from some of the best drivers in NASCAR history. Ironically, Kyle Petty has nine NASCAR victories, but none have come in Petty race cars; those wins came for the Wood Brothers in 1986 and 1987 and Felix Sabates between 1990 and 1995.

Petty's primary role today is that of driver of the No. 45 Petty Enterprises Dodge. He is also chief executive officer of Petty Enterprises, which means he wears many hats, not just the helmet he slides his head into on weekends.

Through the month of September, there were only two top-10s for Petty in 2005. One came early in the season at Bristol Motor Speedway where he scored an eighth-place finish. The second was another eighth at Dover, Delaware, on September 25th. The rest show him mired down in a sea of finishes outside the top 10. His worst showings were a 43rd at

Petty Enterprises driver Jeff Green (43) fights boss Kyle Petty (45) for track position with Rusty Wallace (2) and Bill Elliott (91) close behind.

Petty is one of the most liked individuals in any garage area around the circuit.

Talladega, a 41st at Pocono, and another 41st at Richmond.

Early on, there was no doubt what his career path would be. When your last name is Petty, you're the only son, and your father is known as "The King" of stock car racing, your career is pretty much pre-ordained. Even before he ever drove a race car, Kyle Petty was being touted as a star of the future. He was the talk of racing circles at home and abroad. Surely he would be a chip off the old block, they said.

As a child, Kyle saw stock car racing as nothing more than his father's profession. The cars in the nearby shop were shiny blue with painted numbers on their doors, set up to be turned left around short tracks and superspeedways. He was surrounded by the

Petty's No. 45 Petty Enterprises Dodge is always a sentimental favorite among the fans.

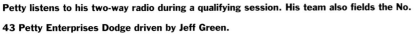

Petty listens to his two-way radio during a qualifying session. His team also fields the No. 43 Petty Enterprises Dodge driven by Jeff Green.

Petty can often be seen sporting a large smile as he walks through the garage area.

sounds of air grinders hitting metal and engines screaming on the dynamometer.

At the start of Speedweeks in 1979, Petty came to Daytona International Speedway with a Dodge Magnum, a discarded NASCAR NEXTEL Cup Series machine his father had used with no success the year before. Although it had a heavy box-like design, the car was perfect for the younger Petty, who entered it in ARCA competition.

Miraculously, Kyle met the media expectations right off the bat. He won the ARCA 200 in his first outing on a closed course. For a brief time, he was the only undefeated stock car driver in America.

A total of 169 races passed before Petty found victory lane in major NASCAR competition in 1986 at Richmond, Virginia. Those seven other victories followed, but none have come in over 10 years.

In an effort to help get Petty Enterprises back on track, a face from the past has returned to Petty Enterprises beginning with the 2006 season. Petty has hired Robbie Loomis, former crew chief for Jeff Gordon, as vice president of race operations. Loomis was Richard Petty's crew chief prior to his retirement from driving in 1992.

Petty says he still enjoys his role as driver, even though he hasn't won a race in quite some time.

"The driving part is still always as much fun, even when you have a bad day driving," Petty says. "It's like we all joke, it's all smoke and mirrors, a bad day driving is still better than having a real job. So, the driving part is still just as much fun. And, there are guys who are stepping aside, Mark and Rusty, obviously. And then you've got myself. And you've got

Sterling, Dale Jarrett, and Ricky Rudd. There's guys that are our age, that are 45 to 50 years old, that yeah, over the next four or five years, not only are we going to step out, we should be stepping out. Because there are guys coming along like the Kasey Kahnes, like the Reed Sorensons, guys like that who are going to be stepping in. You can't just keep taking up a seat forever and ever until the end of time. You've got to let somebody else have a seat.

"I think, from that perspective, yeah you look at it [retirement] and the closer you get to it you look at it. But at the same time, it's not something I think about every day because my main objective right now is to make sure that we build Petty Enterprises back to a state where we can go get young drivers who can come out and be competitive and hopefully compete and win races."

SCOTT RIGGS

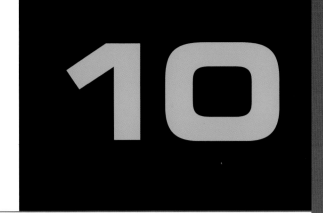

10

Unfortunately for Scott Riggs, driver of the Valvoline/MB2 Motorsports Chevrolet, the top-5 and top-10 finishes simply didn't come as he hoped they would in 2005. There were only three finishes in single digits throughout the majority of the season. He started the season with a fourth-place finish in the season-opening Daytona 500 in February. A ninth-place run at Atlanta in March renewed some of their hope. But it wasn't until Michigan in August that Riggs scored his best finish of the season, which was a second to Jeremy Mayfield in the

Evernham Motorsports Dodge. The remaining events were disappointing, his worst being 41st on the return trip to Daytona in July.

Riggs has enjoyed a rather speedy move into the fast lane, having competed in both the NASCAR Busch Series and NASCAR Craftsman Truck Series. Riggs enjoys the fact he has victories in both of those divisions and used them to pave the way to an invitation to NASCAR's most elite arena.

Even though he hasn't been able to log many top-5 and top-10 finishes, he still possesses the talent to attract some attention

Born:	January 1, 1971, Bahama, North Carolina
Height:	5-8
Weight:	180 lbs

Sponsor	**Valvoline**
Make	**Chevrolet**
Crew Chief	**Rodney Childers**
Team	**MBV Motorsports**

Riggs' MBV Motorsports crew services his Chevrolet with tires and fuel, usually in less than 15 seconds.

from other team owners who want his services.

As a result, Riggs makes some big changes in 2006, as he will be joining Mayfield as a teammate at Evernham Motorsports, taking the No. 10 and sponsor Valvoline to that operation.

Even though the statistics may not show it, Riggs feels he has some good runs in 2005.

"We may not [have been] in the Chase, but we've still got something to prove," Riggs said. "We've known since the beginning of the season that this Valvoline team is capable of a win, and we still believe that. That's why we're going to continue racing as hard as ever to get there.

"We've had some great runs this year but haven't been able to get to the checkered flag and that's what matters. We lost a couple of engines, got collected in other people's wrecks, and missed the setup a few times, but we've been competitive."

Scott Riggs (10) leads drivers Kevin Harvick (29), Travis Kvapil (77), and Joe Nemechek (01) at Bristol Motor Speedway. Riggs has gone winless since joining the NASCAR NEXTEL Cup Series in 2004.

NASCAR NEXTEL Cup Series Series Career Statistics

YEAR	RACES	WINS	TOP 5S	TOP 10S	POLES	TOTAL POINTS	FINAL STANDING	WINNINGS
2004	35	0	1	2	0	3,090	29th	$3,443,350
2005	36	0	2	4	1	2,965	34th	$4,030,685
TOTALS	71	0	3	6	1	6,055		$7,474,035

RICKY RUDD

21

E ven though Ricky Rudd, driver of the Wood Brothers Ford, may admit he's closer to retirement than he once was, he's still having fun doing about the only thing he's ever done in his life. With the addition of friend and former crew chief twice

Born: September 12, 1956, Chesapeake, Virginia

Height: 5-8

Weight: 160 lbs

Sponsor	**Motorcraft**
Make	**Ford**
Crew Chief	**Michael McSwain**
Team	**Wood Brothers Racing**

NASCAR NEXTEL Cup Series Career Statistics

YEAR	RACES	WINS	TOP 5S	TOP 10S	POLES	TOTAL POINTS	FINAL STANDING	WINNINGS
1975	4	0	0	1	0	431	53rd	$4,345
1976	4	0	0	1	0	407	56th	$7,525
1977	25	0	1	10	0	2,810	17th	$68,448
1978	13	0	0	4	0	1,264	32nd	$49,610
1979	28	0	4	17	0	3,642	9th	$146,302
1980	13	0	1	3	0	1,319	32nd	$50,500
1981	31	0	14	17	3	3,991	6th	$381,968
1982	30	0	6	13	2	3,542	9th	$201,130
1983	30	2	7	14	4	3,693	9th	$257,585
1984	30	1	7	16	4	3,918	7th	$476,602
1985	28	1	13	19	0	3,857	6th	$512,441
1986	29	2	11	17	1	3,823	5th	$671,548
1987	29	2	10	13	0	3,742	6th	$653,508
1988	29	1	6	11	2	3,547	11th	$410,954
1989	29	1	7	15	0	3,608	8th	$534,824
1990	29	1	8	15	2	3,601	7th	$573,650
1991	29	1	9	17	1	4,092	2nd	$1,093,765
1992	29	1	9	18	1	3,735	7th	$793,903
1993	30	1	9	14	0	3,644	10th	$752,562
1994	31	1	6	15	1	4,050	5th	$1,044,441
1995	31	1	10	16	2	3,734	9th	$1,337,703
1996	31	1	5	16	0	3,845	6th	$1,503,025
1997	32	2	6	11	0	3,330	17th	$1,975,981
1998	33	1	1	5	0	3,131	22nd	$1,602,895
1999	34	0	3	5	1	2,922	31st	$1,632,011
2000	34	0	12	19	2	4,575	5th	$2,974,970
2001	36	2	14	22	1	4,706	4th	$4,878,027
2002	36	1	8	12	1	4,323	10th	$4,009,380
2003	36	0	4	5	0	3,521	23rd	$3,106,614
2004	36	0	1	3	1	3,615	24th	$3,717,100
2005	36	0	2	9	0	3,667	21st	$4,300,412
TOTALS	875	23	194	373	29	104,085		$36,723,729

Ricky Rudd, a veteran of **NASCAR NEXTEL Cup Series** racing, wheels the No. 21 Wood Brothers Ford. The Wood family has been involved in the sport for over 50 years.

over Michael McSwain, there may be more fun, and more wins, on the horizon.

In 2005, Rudd did manage to produce a few good finishes. The highlights featured a seventh-place finish at Martinsville, an eighth at Texas, a second at Sonoma, California, a seventh at Chicago, and a fourth a Bristol, Tennessee.

Rudd began racing motocross and go karts at a very early age but didn't drive a stock car until he first sat down in a NASCAR NEXTEL Cup Series ride in 1975 at age 18. He took four starts that year with Bill Champion, and one top-10 finish foretold Rudd's potential. In 1976, he started four more events, this time in cars fielded by his father, Al Rudd Sr., and reeled off another top-10 finish—a hint of the

Rudd's Wood Brothers crew has enjoyed a reputation for some of the fastest pit stops over decades. Here they service Rudd's No. 21 Ford.

Rudd is a huge favorite among those in the military. He was sponsored by the U.S. Air Force in 2005.

consistency that would mark his lengthy career. With his family-owned team, Rudd tackled the majority of the schedule in 1977, competing in 25 events, and earned Rookie-of-the-Year honors after finishing 17th in the point standings that season.

Rudd came back to start in 13 races in 1978, garnering results sufficient to land a ride with longtime team owner Junie Donlavey for the full schedule in 1979. He scored two third-place finishes and two fifths in 1979, earning him nearly $150,000. Overall, it was a good learning season for Rudd.

Rudd rests while watching his crew work on his car.

Rudd (21) leads drivers Carl Edwards (99) and Brian Vickers (25), among others, as they battle for track position.

In 1980, back with the Rudd family operation for 13 events, Ricky found himself in a make-or-break situation. Money was running out fast, but one good race could get him noticed by the better-financed teams on the circuit, providing perhaps his only chance to remain an active driver. That October, Rudd entered the National 500 at Lowe's Motor Speedway in a year-old car and qualified on the outside front row. By race's end, Rudd was fourth, finishing behind legends Dale Earnhardt, Cale Yarborough, and Buddy Baker. As hoped, the impressive run caught the notice of several veteran team owners.

Rudd signed with DiGard Racing for the 1981 season, replacing Darrell Waltrip. Even though the results from the DiGard-Rudd union weren't overly impressive, there were definite signs of promise.

Rudd switched to the Richard Childress team in 1982, and his first NASCAR NEXTEL Cup Series victory came the following year at the Budweiser 400 in Riverside, California. Over the next few years, Rudd won six races driving for Bud Moore, two more with Kenny Bernstein, and captured four wins and a second-place finish in

the 1991 NASCAR NEXTEL Cup Series point championship with Rick Hendrick. Since then, he has scored more victories with his own team and with Robert Yates, a longtime friend he joined at the start of the 2000 season. Rudd logged three victories for Yates before he moved over to Wood Brothers Racing at the start of the 2003 season. After two seasons, Rudd is still searching for his first victory with the Woods.

After decades of NASCAR NEXTEL Cup Series racing, Rudd is rather calm, even when he's traveling at speeds nearing 200 miles per hour. He suffered blown engines at California and Charlotte this year, and had an accident at Indianapolis.

Rudd admitted in 2005 that at times he has a hard time keeping his cool when things aren't going well.

"The way our season has gone this year, I'd probably be an emotional wreck if I let it eat at me," Rudd says. "It bothers me, don't get me wrong. Most of the things that have taken us out this year have been really stupid moves by guys, some moves that really don't make sense to me, but I'm not going to change that."

Rudd is all smiles as he listens to a story during a break in the action.

Rudd works his way around a turn while searching for a fast lap.

ELLIOTT SADLER

38

Born: April 30, 1975, Emporia, Virginia

Height: 6-2

Weight: 195 lbs

Sponsor	**M&M's**
Make	**Ford**
Crew Chief	**Kevin Buskirk**
Team	**Robert Yates Racing**

Over the past couple of NASCAR NEXTEL Cup Series season, Elliott Sadler, driver of the Robert Yates Racing Ford, has established himself as a driver to watch, especially on the rescrictor plate tracks such as Daytona and Talladega. He scored an eleventh-place finish in the season-opening Daytona 500, a sixth at Talladega in April, a twenty-first at Daytona in July, and a thirty-fourth after a crash at Talladega on October 2. Still, there were several impressive finishes for Sadler in 2005, but none good enough to get into the Chase for the NASCAR NEXTEL Cup. An eighth at California, a second at Bristol, a ninth at Martinsville, a seventh at Richmond, an eighth at Michigan, and a sixth at Sonoma, California, gave him hope, but a string of worse finishes beginning at Daytona in July systematically dismantled the team's dream of making the Chase.

Sadler has enjoyed going fast since a rather young age. He began racing go karts at age seven. By the time he turned to stock cars at age 18, he had compiled the same winning record as Richard Petty.

Before long, the urge to take his racing to a higher level brought Sadler to NASCAR's Busch Series. In 76 starts in the series, Sadler logged five victories and twelve top-5s. His standout abilities caught the attention of brothers Len and Eddie Wood in 1999.

Wood Brothers Racing and their drivers are storied legends in NASCAR.

Elliott Sadler, driver of the No. 38 Robert Yates Ford, drives one of the most colorful cars on the circuit. Many feel the colors mirror his personality.

Sadler, known for his distinctive Virginia accent, takes a break in the garage area while his crew services his car.

Sadler showed early in his NASCAR NEXTEL Cup Series career that he has the talent to follow in the footsteps of the great drivers of the past, such as Marvin Panch, Chris Turner, and David Pearson. He quickly repaid the Wood brothers' confidence in him with a win at Bristol Motor Speedway in April 2001.

NASCAR NEXTEL Cup Series Career Statistics

YEAR	RACES	WINS	TOP 5S	TOP 10S	POLES	TOTAL POINTS	FINAL STANDING	WINNINGS
1998	2	0	0	0	0	128	---	$45,325
1999	34	0	0	1	0	3,191	24th	$1,589,221
2000	33	0	0	1	0	2,762	29th	$1,578,356
2001	36	1	2	2	0	3,471	20th	$2,683,225
2002	36	0	2	7	0	3,418	23rd	$3,390,690
2003	36	0	2	9	2	3,525	22nd	$3,660,174
2004	36	2	8	14	0	6,024	9th	$5,158,360
2005	36	0	7	12	4	4,084	13th	$5,024,119
TOTALS	249	3	21	46	6	26,603		$23,129,470

Elliott Sadler (38) drops low and passes teammate Dale Jarrett (88) at Michigan International Speedway.

For 2002, Sadler had no wins, two top-5s, and seven top-10s. In 2003, Sadler joined Robert Yates Racing and enjoyed some promising finishes. Victory lane, however, eluded him. In 2004, he recorded his second career win at Texas Motor Speedway on April 4.

For 2005, Sadler was winless through Talladega in October. The week before the Talladega event, crew chief Todd Parrott was asked to move over to Dale Jarrett's Robert Yates operation, leaving Sadler in somewhat of a rebuilding mode for the remainder of the season. Kevin Buskirk was named crew chief

Jamie McMurray (left) enjoys a laugh with Sadler as they relax in the garage area.

Sadler shows his excitement after winning the NEXTEL Cup event at Texas Motor Speedway in the spring of 2004. Note the cowboy hat he wore in victory lane.

Team owner Robert Yates (left) talks with Sadler during a break in the action. Sadler seems rather happy with the top-notch equipment Yates provided for him.

for Sadler. Still, he feels optimistic about his future with his Yates team.

"He's pretty much probably one of the best-kept secrets we've got in the Robert Yates organization," Sadler says of Buskirk. "I just think Todd and Dale had a lot of magic years ago and won a lot of races and ran good and can really maybe fill each other's voids that they've been missing the last year or so. And I think Kevin and I give ourselves a great opportunity to work together, too.

"I think we're gonna continue to on the pace that we're running on and I think that with them being that much better we can kind of leapfrog each other and kind of make our teams better. Instead of one team going in a direction and the other following, I think now we can go our separate ways, learn some things, put it together and make both teams stronger. I really believe that."

Sadler is often seen smiling, whether inside or outside of his Robert Yates Racing Ford.

BORIS SAID

36

Born: September 18, 1962, New York, New York

Height: 6-0

Weight: 180 lbs

Sponsor	**CENTRIX Financial**
Make	**Chevrolet**
Crew Chief	**Frank Stoddard**
Team	**MB/Sutton Motorsports**

Throughout his driving career, Boris Said has spent a great deal of time turning right *and* left. He has spent many years competing in SCCA Trans-Am competition on road courses around the world. He won the SCCA Showroom GT National championship in 1989, 1990 and 1991, as well as the SCCA Trans-Am championship in 2002. Said used that experience as an introduction to NASCAR NEXTEL Cup Series racing, as some of the NASCAR regulars would call upon him to either coach them around such road courses as Sonoma, California, or Watkins Glen, New York. In some cases, they have turned the wheel over to him, as his experience was something no quick lesson could convey.

Said gained NASCAR experience by competing in the NASCAR Craftsman Truck Series in 1997, 1998, and 1999. While there, he compiled one win, two pole positions, six top-5s and nine top-10s.

Also in 1999, Said recorded his first start in NASCAR NEXTEL Cup Series competition for team owner Mark Simo at Watkins Glen, New York. That day, he started second but finished forty-second due to engine problems.

In 2000, he found himself substituting for Jimmy Spencer at Sonoma. The following year, he finished 11th at Sonoma in a car fielded just for him by team owner Doug Bawel. He repeated his entry for Bawel in 2002, but finished 41st due to an accident. He finished 13th at Watkins Glen in August of that year.

In 2003, Said joined MB2 Motorsports as their road course specialist, but he wanted desperately to run ovals on the NASCAR schedule. That didn't come until the 2005 season where he competed frequently in NASCAR NEXTEL Cup Series racing.

"I've got a tough hill to climb, but I've got a great team, and Centrix is a great sponsor," Said offered in *NASCAR Illustrated*. "As far as the package goes, I have Hendrick Motors, I've got the best situation I've ever had.

"I can't wait to get to the road courses. All drivers have egos. When you come to these tracks, and start in the back, it sucks. I can't wait to get to a road course to know I've got a really good chance at a top-5."

Boris Said, driver of the MB/Sutton Motorsports, cut his teeth on road courses. He is now working hard to make himself a name for himself in NASCAR NEXTEL Cup competition.

Said (right) talks with teammate from the 2005 season Scott Riggs before taking to the track.

NASCAR NEXTEL Cup Series Career Statistics

YEAR	RACES	WINS	TOP 5S	TOP 10S	POLES	TOTAL POINTS	FINAL STANDING	WINNINGS
1999	2	0	0	0	0	103	59th	$68,657
2000	1	0	0	0	0	37	71st	$36,940
2001	2	0	0	1	0	272	50th	$124,340
2002	2	0	0	0	0	164	59th	$87,400
2003	2	0	0	1	1	201	55th	$134,680
2004	3	0	0	1	0	302	49th	$252,440
2005	9	0	1	1	0	791	42nd	$1,006,678
TOTALS	21	0	1	4	1	1,870		$1,711,135

TONY STEWART

20

When the 2005 NASCAR NEXTEL Cup Series season began, one of the favorites to win the championship was Tony Stewart, driver of the Joe Gibbs Racing Chevrolet. On several occasions during the season, Stewart fueled that idea by winning in dominant fashion, performing flawlessly on flat tracks such as New Hampshire and Indianapolis. But he was just as good on the high-bank of Daytona, as well as on the road course at Sonoma and Watkins Glen, New York.

Of those 2005 victories, one stood out as the most special of his 24-career victories. He finally won at Indianapolis Motor Speedway, taking the Brickyard 400. It is considered his home track and a place where he tried to win numerous times in Indy car competition.

When Stewart arrived in the NASCAR Winston Cup (now NEXTEL) arena to drive Pontiacs for team owner Joe Gibbs, most everyone billed him as a likely instant winner. The Indiana native had already spent many

Born:	May 20, 1971, Rushville, Indiana
Height:	5-9
Weight:	170 lbs

Sponsor	**Home Depot**
Make	**Chevrolet**
Crew Chief	**Greg Zipadelli**
Team	**Joe Gibbs Racing**

Stewart sits contemplating his strategy just prior to race time.

years winning races in the open-wheel sprint car ranks as well as in the most elite of open-wheel arenas, the Indianapolis 500. With such tremendous talent established so early on, all kinds of offers came his way, but the best came from Gibbs, who is also a past Super Bowl–winning coach with his current team, the Washington Redskins.

Stewart exceeded expectations and began his NASCAR portfolio by breaking the record for wins by a rookie and winning the 1999 Raybestos Rookie of the Year. His first victory came in his 25th start, at Richmond International Raceway in Virginia. By season's end, Stewart and his team were clicking well enough to win back-to-back races at Phoenix, Arizona, and Homestead, Florida.

Perhaps Stewart's most impressive accomplishment of 1999 was racing in both the

Tony Stewart wheels his orange-and-black Joe Gibbs Racing Chevrolet at speed during one of his many events in 2005.

NASCAR NEXTEL Cup Series Career Statistics

YEAR	RACES	WINS	TOP 5S	TOP 10S	POLES	TOTAL POINTS	FINAL STANDING	WINNINGS
1999	34	3	12	21	2	4,774	4th	$3,190,149
2000	34	6	12	23	2	4,570	6th	$3,642,348
2001	36	3	15	22	0	4,763	2nd	$4,941,463
2002	36	3	15	21	4	4,800	1st	$4,695,150
2003	36	2	12	18	1	4,549	7th	$5,227,503
2004	36	2	10	19	0	6,326	6th	$6,221,710
2005	36	5	17	25	3	6,533	1st	$6,987,535
TOTALS	248	24	93	149	12	36,315		$34,905,858

Stewart (white uniform) walks alongside the No. 20 Chevrolet along with his crew as they move the car back to the garage after qualifying.

Dale Jarrett (left) spends a few minutes with Stewart, possibly talking about Stewart's open-wheel Sprint car career.

Coca-Cola World 600 at Charlotte and the Indianapolis 500 on the same day.

After an exhaustive 1,100 miles of high-speed magic, he finished fourth in the 600 at Charlotte Motor Speedway and ninth in the 500 at Indianapolis Motor Speedway.

In 2000, many looked to Stewart to pull off the rare accomplishment of winning a Winston Cup championship the very next year after capturing rookie honors. Unfortunately, Stewart got off to a slow start in his sophomore season, ultimately finishing a respectable sixth in points while teammate Bobby Labonte captured his first Cup championship.

The next year, Tony Stewart enjoyed his best season to date. He started 2001 off with a victory in the Bud Shoot-Out, a special non-points event for pole-position winners. In June, he was a winner on the road course at Sears Point, California. He followed that performance with another victory at Richmond and also pulled off a win at the demanding high-banked short track of Bristol Motor Speedway. In the end, he finished second to Jeff Gordon in the overall championship hunt after coming on strong at the end when others suffered mechanical failures.

For the second time in his career, Stewart attempted the Charlotte/Indy double duty in 2001. He again finished strong, coming in sixth in the 500 and third in the 600 at Charlotte. He elected not to do so in 2002, knowing the championship race needed his full attention.

That year, Stewart put together his first career NASCAR NEXTEL Cup Series championship with 3 victories, 15 top-5s, and 21 top-10s in 36 starts.

For 2003, Stewart enjoyed a win at Pocono, Pennsylvania, and several races where he challenged for the win but settled for top-5 finishes.

In 2004, Stewart suffered through a hot-and-cold season, winning races at Chicago and Watkins Glen, New York.

In 2005, Stewart certainly established himself as a solid championship contender, especially during the second half of the season, he logged five wins, nine top-5s and eleven top-10s. Those are the kind of numbers needed to have any hope at winning a championship.

Stewart won the 2005 NASCAR NEXTEL Cup Championship and feels his team has found a few secrets that others have not yet discovered.

"It just shows how competitive the series is now," Stewart says. "You look at Formula One and how dominant Ferrari was for so many years. They found something that nobody else found. That's the way this series is getting. We all have the same rules to go by. But once you find a package, especially with the new rules package this year, the Roush and Hendrick teams found that combination early and it took us a little longer to find it.

"Now that we have, we're a contender again."

Stewart (20) leads Mike Bliss (80) and Ryan Newman (12) through a turn while battling for track position. Stewart enjoys all types of racing and also campaigns on the Sprint Car circuit when his schedule permits.

Stewart's trademark after winning in 2005 was to climb the fence to the flag stand, as he did here after his win at New Hampshire in July 2005.

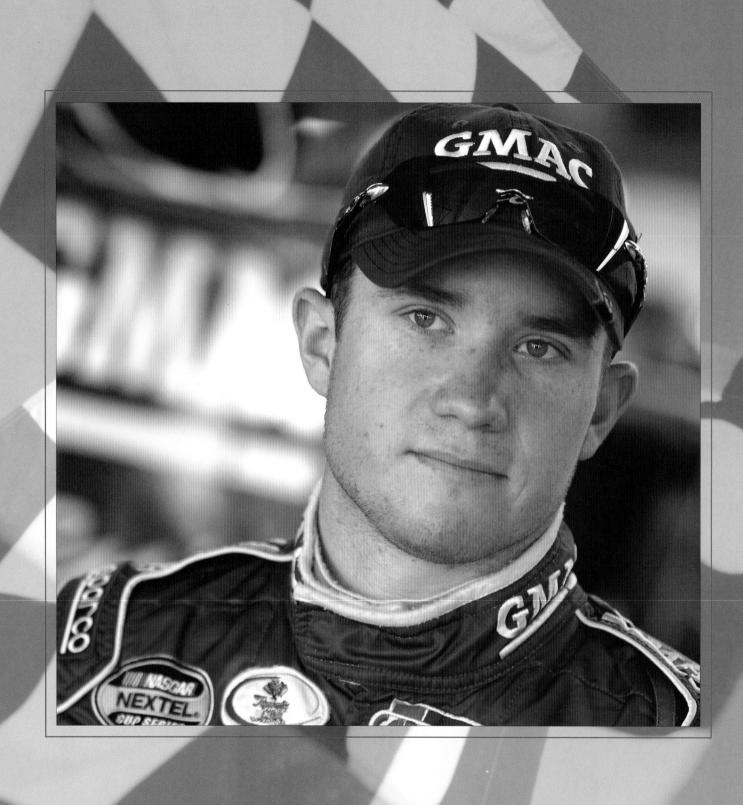

BRIAN VICKERS

25

During the 2005 season, Brian Vickers was in his second season of learning the ins and outs of NASCAR NEXTEL Cup Series racing. As in 2004, the competition level makes NASCAR racing one of the toughest forms of auto racing in the world.

His road to NEXTEL Cup racing has been a long, calculated journey. For Vickers, driver of the Hendrick Motorsports Chevrolet, racing became his passion in 1994 when he began racing go karts in hopes of a championship or two down the road. He accomplished that feat three times, in 1995, 1996, and 1997. Along with his world karting championship, Vickers was a four-time North Carolina karting champion, traveling the state from his Thomasville home. Coincidentally, that was about the time the aspiring young driver met

Born: October 24, 1983, Thomasville, North Carolina

Height: 5-9

Weight: 155 lbs

Sponsor	**GMAC**
Make	**Chevrolet**
Crew Chief	**Lance McGrew**
Team	**Hendrick Motorsports**

Brian Vickers, driver of the Hendrick Motorsports Chevrolet, leads teammate Jimmie Johnson (48) and Kurt Busch (97) in the Roush Racing Ford.

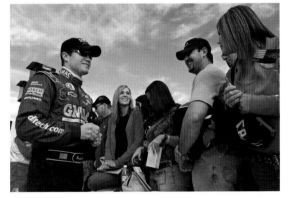

Vickers enjoys visiting with his fans at all of the NEXTEL Cup events. He is helping to bring a younger crowd to the sport of stock car racing.

NASCAR NEXTEL Cup Series driver Terry Labonte—now a teammate at Hendrick Motorsports—who was a neighbor a short half-mile down the road. Labonte ended up offering Vickers a ride, but it wasn't in a race car—it was in the back seat of the Labonte's passenger car en route to junior high school.

Vickers continued in a variety of stock car racing divisions, enjoying success in virtually all of them. A family-operated NASCAR Busch Series operation ensued in 2000, and Vickers eventually worked his way to entering 21 events the following season, posting one top-10 finish. His efforts attracted the eye of then fellow driver Ricky Hendrick (son of team owner Rick Hendrick), and the two soon

NASCAR NEXTEL Cup Series Career Statistics

YEAR	RACES	WINS	TOP 5S	TOP 10S	POLES	TOTAL POINTS	FINAL STANDING	WINNINGS
2004	36	0	0	4	2	3,521	25th	$3,044,900
2005	36	0	5	10	1	3,487	17th	$3,982,133
TOTALS	72	0	5	14	3	7,368		$7,027,033

Vickers' crew swarms around his Hendrick Motorsports Chevrolet with tires and fuel in hand. Many four-tire stops are performed in just over 13 seconds.

struck up a friendship. When Ricky Hendrick elected to retire from driving after a hard crash, Vickers was tapped as his replacement, setting the wheels of opportunity in motion.

Vickers won the 2003 NASCAR Busch Series championship in a Hendrick Chevrolet, winning three events.

Also that season, Vickers made his NASCAR NEXTEL Cup Series debut at Charlotte in October. He also made four more starts and qualified in the top-5 in four of the five races. His best finish that year was 13th at Phoenix.

In 2004, Vickers best finishes were an eighth at Richmond, a ninth at Michigan, and a ninth at Daytona.

Vickers makes good use of a few tools in the garage area as he finds a place to prop his feet during a break in the action.

Vickers (25) leads teammate Kyle Busch (5), along with Jeff Burton (31) and Carl Edwards (99), as they race for position.

Vickers sports his sunglasses as he relaxes in the garage area between practice sessions.

Vickers enjoyed several impressive finishes in 2005, such as a sixth at Bristol, a fifth at Talladega, a second at Michigan, a fourth at New Hampshire, and a third at Richmond. Vickers feels he and his team have greatly improved.

"We really have," Vickers says. "This team has really come around and I'm so proud of everybody. It takes everybody from the engine shop, to the bodies to Lance [McGrew, crew chief] and all the guys to really make it happen."

Vickers studies the track through his windshield, preparing for another NASCAR NEXTEL Cup Series event.

RUSTY WALLACE

2

Rusty Wallace will look upon the 2005 season as bittersweet. He ran well enough to enter the Chase for the NASCAR NEXTEL Cup Series, but the 2005 season is his last, as he will retire at the end of the year.

Few drivers in any type of auto racing have enjoyed the fan following that Wallace has enjoyed. On top of his game or fighting his way back from the rear of the pack, his fans are loyal and devoted.

Wallace's first venture into NASCAR racing came at Atlanta Motor Speedway in 1980. The young Missourian wasn't supposed to have much of a chance, but that day Wallace made the most of his ride. He was leading with 29

Born:	August 14, 1956, Fenton, Missouri
Height:	6-0
Weight:	185 lbs

Sponsor	**Miller Lite**
Make	**Dodge**
Crew Chief	**Larry Carter**
Team	**Penske Racing**

laps to go when Dale Earnhardt passed him for the win. Wallace held on for second place, and his sensational debut was a sure sign of things to come.

Wallace won rookie honors in USAC competition in 1979 and was the 1983 ASA champion. He established himself as a strong threat to win anywhere he raced and entered select Cup races. In NASCAR NEXTEL Cup Series racing, Wallace was Rookie of the Year. His first victory came in the 76th start of his career, on April 6, 1986, at Bristol Motor Speedway.

Within just two years, Wallace was contending for the championship, finishing as runner-up for the 1988 title by only 24 points. A year later, after a season-long battle with Earnhardt, Wallace was crowned the 1989 NASCAR NEXTEL Cup Series champion, inching out The Intimidator by 12 points.

Wallace's best years for wins came in 1993 and 1994, when he logged 18 wins in 61 starts.

Over a 17-year period, Wallace has collected 54 NASCAR NEXTEL Cup Series victories, 36 of them with Penske's organization.

The 2005 season was one of Wallace's best and a great way end an illustrious career.

"A lot of people have asked me why I'm retiring because I'm still winning and running good," Wallace says. "I guess I'd have to say the answer to that question is that I just want to go out on top. That's the way I'd like for my driving career to end."

NASCAR NEXTEL Cup Series Career Statistics

YEAR	RACES	WINS	TOP 5S	TOP 10S	POLES	TOTAL POINTS	FINAL STANDING	WINNINGS
1980	2	0	1	1	0	291	---	$22,760
1981	4	0	0	1	0	399	---	$12,895
1982	3	0	0	0	0	186	---	$7,655
1983	0	0	0	0	0	0	---	$1,100
1984	30	0	2	4	0	3,316	14th	$195,927
1985	28	0	2	8	0	2,867	19th	$233,670
1986	29	2	4	16	0	3,757	6th	$557,354
1987	29	2	9	16	1	3,818	5th	$690,652
1988	29	6	19	23	2	4,464	2nd	$1,411,567
1989	29	6	13	20	4	4,176	1st	$2,247,950
1990	29	2	9	16	2	3,676	6th	$954,129
1991	29	2	9	14	2	3,582	10th	$502,073
1992	29	1	5	12	1	3,556	13th	$657,925
1993	30	10	19	21	3	4,446	2nd	$1,702,154
1994	31	8	17	20	2	4,207	3rd	$1,914,072
1995	31	2	15	19	0	4,240	5th	$1,642,837
1996	31	5	8	18	0	3,717	7th	$1,665,315
1997	32	1	8	12	1	3,598	9th	$1,705,625
1998	33	1	15	21	4	4,501	4th	$2,667,889
1999	34	1	7	16	4	4,155	8th	$2,454,050
2000	34	4	12	20	9	4,544	7th	$3,621,468
2001	36	1	8	14	0	4,481	7th	$4,788,652
2002	36	0	7	17	1	4,574	7th	$4,090,050
2003	36	0	2	12	0	3,850	14th	$3,766,744
2004	36	1	3	11	0	3,960	16th	$4,447,300
2005	36	0	8	17	0	6,140	8th	$4,868,976
TOTALS	706	55	202	349	36	90,501		$46,830,789

MICHAEL WALTRIP

For the majority of the 2005 NASCAR NEXTEL Cup Series season, Michael Waltrip has known he would be leaving the Dale Earnhardt, Inc. operation. The question mark has been where he would go after his tenure was complete.

That mystery was solved in September when he announced he would be joining Bill Davis Racing with NAPA Auto Parts as his primary sponsor.

The younger brother of three-time NASCAR NEXTEL Cup Series champion Darrell Waltrip, Michael Waltrip is probably best known for his victory in the 2001 Daytona 500. It came in the 462nd start of a career that dates back to 1985. The victory will forever be overshadowed by the death of Dale Earnhardt on the final lap. Coincidentally, Waltrip was driving a Chevrolet owned by Earnhardt. He was in the lead, two positions ahead of the legendary driver when the fatal crash occurred.

Waltrip returned to Daytona in July of that year and finished second to DEI teammate Dale Earnhardt Jr. in the 400-mile event. Waltrip now has over 500 starts in a career that also includes 21 top-5s, 85 top-10s, and 2 pole

Born:	April 30, 1963, Owensboro, Kentucky
Height:	6-5
Weight:	210 lbs

Sponsor	**NAPA**
Make	**Chevrolet**
Crew Chief	**Tony Gibson**
Team	**DEI**

Michael Waltrip, driver of the Dale Earnhardt, Inc. Chevrolet, is fun to watch each time he visits victory lane.

NASCAR NEXTEL Cup Series Career Statistics

YEAR	RACES	WINS	TOP 5S	TOP 10S	POLES	TOTAL POINTS	FINAL STANDING	WINNINGS
1985	5	0	0	0	0	395	49th	$9,540
1986	28	0	0	0	0	2,853	19th	$108,767
1987	29	0	0	1	0	2,840	20th	$205,370
1988	29	0	1	3	0	2,949	18th	$240,400
1989	29	0	0	5	0	3,067	18th	$249,233
1990	29	0	5	10	0	3,251	16th	$395,507
1991	29	0	4	12	2	3,254	15th	$440,812
1992	29	0	1	2	0	2,825	23rd	$410,545
1993	30	0	0	5	0	3,291	17th	$529,923
1994	31	0	2	10	0	3,512	12th	$706,426
1995	31	0	2	8	0	3,601	12th	$898,338
1996	31	0	1	11	0	3,535	14th	$1,182,811
1997	32	0	0	6	0	3,173	18th	$1,138,599
1998	32	0	0	5	0	3,340	17th	$1,508,680
1999	34	0	1	3	0	2,974	29th	$1,701,160
2000	34	0	1	1	0	2,792	27th	$1,689,421
2001	36	1	3	3	0	3,159	24th	$3,411,644
2002	36	1	4	10	0	3,985	14th	$2,829,180
2003	36	2	8	11	0	3,934	15th	$4,463,485
2004	36	0	2	9	0	3,878	20th	$4,245,690
2005	36	0	3	7	1	3,452	25th	$4,375,088
TOTALS	642	4	38	122	3	66,060		$30,740,619

positions. Waltrip captured a second career victory in 2002, and once again the trophy was earned at the famous Daytona International Speedway. Waltrip's win in the Pepsi 400 that July supplied him with the encouragement he needed for continued success with DEI.

In 2003, Waltrip scored his second career Daytona 500 in a rain-shortened event. He

Michael Waltrip (15) often found himself well out front of the others who raced against him. Unfortunately, the end statistics didn't show any official victories. He was, however, victorious in a special qualifying event prior to the season-opening Daytona 500 in February 2005.

Martin Truex, Jr. (left) stops by to visit with Waltrip in the NASCAR NEXTEL Cup Series garage area.

followed that win by taking the checkered flag at Talladega Superspeedway in October to help the DEI cars dominate those two tracks.

Waltrip fell on a winless streak through 23 events in 2004 and was well out of position to enter the final 10 events with a shot at the championship.

In 2005, Waltrip showed he could post some good runs, including a seventh-place finish at Atlanta, a sixth at Texas, a second at Phoenix, a third at Talladega, a ninth at Richmond, a fifth at Pocono, and a seventh at Michigan.

On the other end of the spectrum, Waltrip endured many finishes out of the top-10, his worst finish of the season, 42nd, coming during the

Since 2001, Waltrip has driven the dark-blue-and-yellow colors of the No. 15 Chevrolet fielded by Dale Earnhardt, Inc. Waltrip is always a favorite among drivers and fans.

second visit to Talladega. Early in the race, his car barrel-rolled during a multi-car accident in Turn 2. Fortunately, Waltrip was uninjured in the crash.

Waltrip is looking forward to a new start with Davis in 2006.

"We decided the best thing we could do is make an association with Bill Davis Racing for 2006, and that gives us time to figure out what '07 and '08 and beyond looks like," Waltrip said in *NASCAR Scene*. "We're going to go forward with our own shop and we'll see how that develops.

"It's hard to compete on this level against guys that have five or six teams when you only have one. We feel like the infusion of fresh people and more money will make a difference at Bill Davis Racing, maybe more so than anywhere else."

Waltrip draws a large group of media members each time he gives interviews. The Kentucky native always offers great quotes.

SCOTT WIMMER

22

Born:	January 26, 1976, Wausau, Wisconsin
Height:	6-0
Weight:	180 lbs

Sponsor	**CAT**
Make	**Dodge**
Crew Chief	**Frank Stoddard**
Team	**Bill Davis Racing**

Scott Wimmer, driver of the Bill Davis Racing Dodge, is slowly becoming more accustomed to NASCAR NEXTEL Cup Series racing. Wimmer has driven for Bill Davis Racing throughout the past five seasons. His best-career finish came in the 2004 Daytona 500, where he captured third place.

Even though relatively new to the world of NASCAR NEXTEL Cup Series racing, Wimmer has certainly shown promise since joining the circuit as a rookie at the beginning of the 2004 season.

Wimmer ran three full seasons in the NASCAR Busch Series with his best championship finish being a third in 2002. He won four races in that division in 2002 at Dover, Delaware; Memphis, Tennessee; Phoenix, Arizona; and Homestead, Florida. The year before, he finished 11th in the NASCAR Busch Series championship and was runner-up to Greg Biffle for Rookie-of-the-Year honors.

In 2000, Wimmer logged one NASCAR NEXTEL Cup Series start, finishing 22nd at Atlanta in his first start. He logged three starts in 2002, with a 19th at Phoenix being his best of the season.

When Ward Burton elected to end his driving relationship with Davis in 2003, Wimmer was tapped to take the ride with four races remaining in the season. All the while, he continued running the NASCAR Busch Series, where he finished ninth in points and scored a victory at Pikes Peak Raceway.

In 2005, Wimmer struggled to log top-10 finishes. His best finish, 14th, came at Bristol Motor Speedway in August.

In late October of 2005, Wimmer was notified that he would not be with the Davis team for 2006. It was very late in the year to get the word that he would not be back. Only two weeks earlier, Wimmer was told he was set for another season.

"I was dissapointed at first, then I started looking on the Internet and looking at papers and I saw there are good rides yet, so it's not the end of the world," he said. "I've never gone through getting released from a team, I've only driven for my father and Bill Davis, so hopefully I can get with somebody that's a real competitive team, runs real strong and can fit in there real well" *(NASCAR Scene).*

Scott Wimmer (22) leads a large group of drivers aiming to take his position away.

Wimmer smiles as he stands in the NASCAR NEXTEL Cup Series garage area.

NASCAR NEXTEL Cup Series Career Statistics

YEAR	RACES	WINS	TOP 5S	TOP 10S	POLES	TOTAL POINTS	FINAL STANDING	WINNINGS
2004	35	0	1	2	0	3,198	27th	$3,675,880
2005	36	0	0	0	0	3,122	32nd	$3,682,979
TOTALS	71	0	1	2	0	6,320		$7,358,859

INDEX